DATE DUE			

Football's Modular Offense

A Flexible System of Attack

Football's Modular Offense

A Flexible System of Attack

John Durham

Parker Publishing Company
West Nyack, New York

796.3322
D 93t
130668
Jan. 1985

Library of Congress Cataloging in Publication Data
Durham, John W.,
    Football's modular offense.
    Includes index.
    1. Football–Offense. 2.Football–Coaching   I. Title.
GV951.8.D87 1984   796.332'2   83-10532

ISBN 0-13-324160-2

Printed in the United States of America

For my wife, Nadine

How This Book Will Help You

In the last decade the most significant technical trends in football have been the refinement of individual defensive techniques and the development of team defensive play. Modern defenses are so thoroughly coached that it has become difficult to overpower or fool them. Today's offensive coach finds himself on the horns of a dilemma. He faces many defensive fronts, charges, coverages, and stunts that are so well executed that they demand a large arsenal of offensive weapons. Conversely, the system of offense he needs seems too complex to teach well to his players. There simply isn't enough time to meet all the requirements.

The Modular Offense solves the problem faced by the offensive coach. This flexible system focuses on the happy medium between simplicity and complexity, using a method of offensive organization. This book demonstrates how to take what the defense gives and set up a specific game plan for a particular opponent, how to adjust the modular system to suit team personnel, and how to tailor a system of offense to individual needs.

The Modular Offense, like all practical inventions, was born of necessity. It is based on a number of simple building blocks, or modules, which can be combined to provide an infinite number of combinations of offensive sets, formations, motions, and plays. Alignment modules consist of formation direction, wing-flank formations, deep back sets, and motion and shifting supplements. Running play modules consist of line blocking patterns, on-the-line calls, backfield actions, and quarterback audibles. Passing game modules include protection schemes for the line, passing actions for the quarterback and deep backs, and combination routes for the receivers.

All these possibilities are overwhelming if considered in total. The enduring principle, however, is that simplicity is the foundation of the offense. It is remarkable how few assignments and techniques need to be taught to develop a flexible system of attack.

If your team has a hard running fullback who is effective in the off tackle hole, and you anticipate facing well coached reading 52 defenses, you may combine a misdirection play from the 50 Series with the tackle trap blocking module. A good counter play can be refined with an initial fullback fake, employing a tackle trap which tends to confuse the reads of the linebackers.

The Modular Offense provides great help to offensive coaches in its use of the blocking patterns for the line in a running game. Prior to using this flexible system, the blocking pattern was tied into the play number for each specific backfield action and play number, with necessary changes made on the line. Now a word designates a blocking pattern for the line. That module is combined with a play number designating backfield action. Because there are very few major modules in line run play assignments, this is a simpler way to teach and practice line play. At the same time it increases the scope of offense tremendously.

Backfield actions for all the series in the Modular Offense are designed with flow charts for all five backfield positions, while all blocking modules assign blocks for the wings, slots, and flankers in all possible positions. This means that there are a tremendous number of ways to combine backfield actions with the best possible blocking schemes to meet a given situation. The passing game is just as flexible. The pass action is combined with a desirable protection module and play fake, or set up action, by the quarterback, allowing great flexibility.

An example of increased efficiency in the passing game is the use of the misdirection pass. A misdirection pass can be thrown from nearly any backfield action. The best running series for a particular season can be selected, and the misdirection pass thrown from it. For maximum protection and a better chance for a run by the quarterback, the *Boot* module can be used, in which both ends block and a single receiver is released. If more receivers are wanted, the *Waggle* module can be used, in which both ends are in the pattern. The pattern combination can also be varied for this pass play, achieving maximum effectiveness in a relatively simple way.

The best thing about this system of attack is that it is *fun* but fundamental; researching it and creating the seasonal and game plans are exhilarating. Even the football purists who are the "block 'em better" men will find that the basic fundamentals of this system are the leavening element in the teaching process. Most of the excitement is still ahead however. The surface of this intriguing method of attack has not yet been scratched.

CONTENTS

chapter *1*

The Evolution of the Modular Offense

There are two fundamental ways to beat the defense. First, you may have better personnel than your opponent. Second, you may coach your players in technique and assignment better than your counterpart does. In most high school situations it is difficult to maintain the former advantage. In recent years well coached defenses have minimized the second possible advantage. Somewhere means must be found to give the offense a technical advantage. It is helpful to examine the evolution of football offense during the last thirty years.

Rise and Fall of the Option Offense

The option offense has cycled in and out of football popularity since the 1940s. It has been very effective with each new "wrinkle" of the cycle, but defensive coaches have discovered how to teach their perimeter players to neutralize the option. There are many forms of effective defense against the option attack, and a good defensive team probably has several ways to attack opponents who run the attack. The most important factor in successful option defense is the current slow play technique of the defensive end, which forces the quarterback to make his pitch-keep decision as late as possible. If the perimeter is properly played, the rest of the defense forces the dive (first phase) hard, and this seemingly devastating offense may fail to move the ball. It is no longer a big play offense, but it still is a high risk offense, with errant pitches and the inevitable fumbles caused by handing off close to the line of scrimmage.

Limitations of the Power Attack

The effectiveness of the power attack is achieved by knocking the defensive front off the ball, leading with one or two backs, and running directly at the defenders. This form of offense is limited by defensive linemen schooled in neutralizing blocks, and by linebackers who read keys and attack the offense aggressively. An example of the evolution of the defense against the power teams is the way the traditional isolation play is defensed today. The "Iso" involves a double team on a defensive lineman and a back leading through on a linebacker. When the linebacker sees the lineman in front of him block to his inside, he fills the hole aggressively and attacks the blocker in the backfield, destroying the running back's path. Keys and reads by the defensive front are very good today, and this reduces the effectiveness of this once consistent ball control form of attack.

Misdirection

Teams that featured misdirection and traps experienced great success in the past. Presently defenders are taught to close traps so well that there isn't anyone to trap. The recent trend is to jam all the blockers on the line of scrimmage, freeing the unblocked linebackers to step up into the trap hole.

With the increased emphasis on the skilled positions in recent years, passing offenses have enjoyed great success. Even though passing is a much greater supplementary weapon than it has ever been, few high school teams are able to consistently make the passing game the predominant part of their offense. Variations in coverages and improved pass rush techniques have served to limit the passing teams.

Successful Offensive Approaches

There are many ways to move the football, and a study of the perennially successful modern offensive teams yields several common principles. First among these principles is that all good offensive teams are fundamentally sound. That is just as true today as it was in the days of Stagg; it is one factor in the game that has not changed. There are some interesting technical innovations, however, which should be investigated.

Power teams have revised their approach, and feature an advanced "run for daylight" concept. They are using versions of the old Lombardi power sweep in which they stretch the defensive front, recognize the soft spot in the pursuit, then accelerate through it. This approach is used in the off tackle and sweep plays. *I* formation teams set the tailback deeper than previously, so that he can read the defense and accelerate through the soft spot. He literally creates his own counters by looking for the soft spot and taking advantage of defensive pursuit.

Option teams generally predetermine the dive phase of the option sequence and have several ways to predetermine the other phases of the attack, including various blocking patterns at the corner.

Trapping teams have developed alternative blocking schemes with combination blocks, folds, and loops, which enables the back to run for the daylight wherever it develops.

Passing teams have devised successful methods of reading the pass coverage, enabling them to launch the pass into the most sparsely defended area.

Almost all offensive systems feature some aspects of all the other systems. A good team may be predominantly a power team, but it usually does some trapping, features some facets of the option attack, and almost always has a strong passing attack.

The Challenge

Following the foregoing analysis to its logical conclusion, everything must be done well. Within the scope of that "everything" lie five or six complete offensive systems. It is impossible to learn that much on any level of play. The challenge is to engineer a system which includes almost all of the facets of the successful attack as discussed. This offense must lend itself to adjustment on a yearly basis, and to a lesser degree on a game by game basis, according to team personnel and the defensive style of the opponents.

A System to Meet the Challenge

A system of play can be designed that encompasses run-for-daylight power, trapping, and some options. A passing game can be built which stretches the defense the entire width of the field, and which can get the ball deep, between the deep coverage and the linebackers and underneath the linebackers. This passing attack can be executed from running play fakes and without running play fakes.

To create the desired passing capability, one position is designated as a constant wingback or flanker with that player drilled as a blocker and receiver, eliminating him as a running back. The two remaining running backs must do the work of three backs, so they are in many different sets. In order to control the strength of the defense, wingbacks are moved to different positions with ends tight, flexed, or split. To avoid communicating intentions and allowing opponents to read formations for tip-offs, you can shift backs and ends and motion the backs. This will also help to weaken the strength of the defense.

The most critical requirement of this offense is varying the blocking patterns to best attack the many defensive fronts, and to conform to different play patterns. Linemen must make calls on the line of scrimmage, enabling them to change blocking assignments to handle stemming and stunting defenses.

Simplicity of Communications

Simplicity of communications is the cornerstone of the Modular Offense. It takes one word to set the wingback-flanker and the line. A second word (actually a letter) sets the two running backs. Sometimes a third word is used for certain combinations or further modifications. A single word is used to designate any kind of motion. A two-digit number is used to identify a running play or play fake. The first digit designates the general flow of the backs, while the second digit indicates the approximate area of penetration. Another word indicates the blocking *module* which determines the scheme used by the line, and possibly one or two backs, to block the defense.

There are literally infinite combinations of blocking modules with play action modules. The season begins with a list of possibilities based on personnel and the defensive styles a coach anticipates confronting. Each week the possibilities are refined on a game-by-game basis. The Modular Offense is multiple offense simply and effectively taught.

A Typical Modular Offense Play

An example of a play from the Modular Offense is *B Star Split, Float, 55 Wham, on Red.* This play is illustrated in Diagram 1-1.

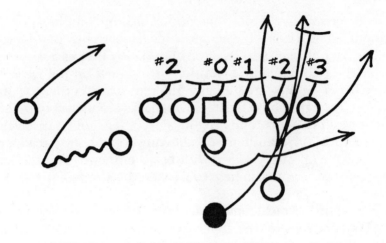

DIAGRAM 1-1: *B Star Split, Float, 55 Wham, on Red*

The *B* indicates the set of the two running backs; *Star* tells the line to align in a right formation and sets the wingback to our left; *Split* moves the split end 10 yards outside his tackle; *Float* puts the wingback in motion away from formation. The number *55* indicates the backfield action and the hole to be hit; *Wham* determines the blocking; and *Red* is the starting count. A shift can be made to the desired formation—shift twice to it, or line up in it directly by using a simple code.

If this sounds interesting, read on.

chapter 2

Fundamentals of the Modular Offense

The most innovative technical system of football is worth little without proper execution of the fundamentals. A sophisticated offense is based on a few fundamentals used in various combinations.

The Drive Block

One block is used for the running game: the drive block. By teaching the blocker to target different areas on the defender according to the defender's position, the flow of the play, and the desired blocking scheme, an offense is built. The blocker is coached to run through his opponent, for the biggest problem in blocking is that football players are so intent on striking a hard blow that they overextend themselves and cannot follow through, losing the block quickly. If the blocker understands the concept of running through the target, he will keep his feet moving and under his hips, which will allow him to follow through with his block. Because of concern with body balance and follow through, coaches allow the blocker to teach himself how to uncoil his body on contact. No mention is made of this uncoiling of the body.

An offensive lineman chooses his target area by running through the hole side hip of the defensive lineman he is assigned to block. Exception is taken to that situation when the defensive lineman is aligned in the gap to the offensive lineman's inside. In that case, the lineman runs through the far hip of the defender in order to break the penetration. If the blocker is attacking a defender other than a lineman, he runs through the hole side armpit.

The post blocker for the double team blocks the hip of the lineman and the armpit of the linebacker opposite the hole side, while the drive blocker on the double team blocks the hole side hip or armpit. Defenders on the line of scrimmage are treated as down lineman.

An offensive lineman on the side of a play fake pass or a sprint out pass blocks as on a drive block, unless there is no lineman in his area. In this case he will block a linebacker or help out to the inside.

Conventional Pass Blocking

Conventional pass blocking by a lineman requires him to get set with the weight on the balls of the feet and the chin over the hips. The blocker must stay in front of the defender; perfect position means he is nose up on the defender, and there is a line drawn to the passer that is perpendicular to the blocker's hips. As the defender approaches the offensive pass blocking lineman, the blocker strikes out with his fists at the sternum of the rusher. The blocker is not allowed to extend his body when he strikes out with his fists. He stays nose up with the rushing defender and strikes the rusher when he closes, to create separation. If the rusher gets to the blocker's hip, the blocker must then drive block by running through the far armpit.

Techniques of Back Blocking

Backs are taught to block by running through the hole side armpit of the defender. The back is taught to pass block by taking two quick steps into the rusher and striking out with the fists when he closes. When the back breaks the charge of the rusher, he remains nose to nose in front of the rusher, striking out with his fists when the defender closes, making certain not to overextend. If the rusher gets on the hip of the blocker, the block becomes a drive block and the target is the far hip of the defender. Because the pass rusher gathers so much momentum by the time he gets into the backfield, the blocker must use two steps and strike to break his charge.

Ball Carrying Fundamentals

Ball carrying fundamentals are often overlooked by football coaches. The ball carrier takes the ball with the inside forearm parallel to the ground and the elbow at armpit level. The other arm is extended parallel to the ground at belt level. The ball carrier must learn to maintain his balance while running. Most young running backs tend to overextend and run with too much body lean.

The runner is coached to approach all collisions with his hips down and under the chin, with the knees high, and with both hands on the ball. The index and middle fingers envelope the tips of the ball. In the open field the ball carrier grips the ball securely so that his hand is on the end of the ball and the other end is lodged in the armpit.

The most important fundamental for the ball carrier is to keep the feet moving. There is a tendency to stop the feet on collision; the ball carrier who overcomes that habit will break many tackles.

Carrying the Ball

In the Modular Offense, the quarterback takes the ball from the center in the old-fashioned way. Although coaches favoring this technique are in the minority, they think it makes ball handling easier. The quarterback has his thumbs together with pressure on the buttocks of the center. His hands are inserted about wrist deep in the center's crotch. The center has the laces toward the right sideline if the quarterback is right handed (opposite for the left-handed quarterback). The center keeps both hands on the ball with the thumbs together on the top seam, and tilts it up slightly. The center turns the ball over and steps forward, simultaneously snapping the ball to the quarterback.

The quarterback handles the ball at belt level in a plane parallel to the ground. He makes handoffs by focusing his eyes on the pocket of the running back and extending the ball smoothly with the far hand, sliding it to the far hip of the ball carrier.

The quarterback passes the ball by rolling his hips and shoulders hard, pointing the belt buckle at the target. He steps with his front foot in the direction of the target. He throws on the run, or from a fixed position. He is drilled to put the proper touch on the ball for all passing situations. He throws the soft underneath passes that the short receivers can handle easily, the sharp passes into the intermediate zones over the top of the linebackers and underneath the deep coverage, and the deep passes with lots of air underneath so the receivers can run under them and make the reception.

Stance for the Modular Offense

Wingbacks and running backs (except for tailbacks) align in a three point stance with the feet parallel and very little weight forward. From this position they are able to come out of the stance and step laterally in either direction or at any angle to the line of scrimmage. The feet are about shoulder width apart, and the buttocks are nearly even with the head.

Tailbacks are in an upright stance with the hands just above the knees. The feet are even and shoulder width apart. The heels are on the ground and the weight is concentrated on the balls of the feet. This stance permits the tailback to start well in any direction except straight ahead. The upright tailback can also read the blocking patterns easily.

The flanker aligns in an upright stance with the inside foot back and the hands on the hips. His vision to the inside is better with the upright stance and the inside foot back.

The offensive lineman uses a four-point stance with the feet parallel and shoulder width apart. The heels are slightly raised off the ground, enabling the lineman to step laterally, straight ahead, or at any angle to the line of scrimmage. The fingers are on the ground. This square stance makes for good balance.

The quarterback's stance incorporates a slight forward bend at the waist, with the feet at shoulder width. He should not be crouched so low that he has to rise to carry out his ball handling duties.

You are now prepared to start talking the Modular Offense.

chapter 3

Coaching Points for the Modular Offense

The Modular Offense can be tailored each season to fit your team personnel. It can be adjusted in a variety of ways. If you have a running quarterback, you can arrange this offense to take maximum advantage of that. If your trigger man is strictly a passer, you can adjust the offense to take advantage of that factor. The personnel requirements of the offense are very flexible.

Personnel and Positions

Do not take your poorest or heaviest lineman and make him your center. He has to snap the ball and probably has the most difficult blocking assignments on the squad. Guards and tackles are blockers, with the guards being a bit more mobile. Linemen's talents, such as straight ahead, draw, and trap blockers, can be used according to the manner in which the offense is implemented.

Depending on the blocking and receiving ability of the ends, you can employ two tight ends, one tight end and a split end, or two split ends. A good athlete with some throwing ability can be developed for quarterback, but many kinds of body types and numerous levels of ability can be accommodated.

A coach may designate a Z back who is a combination wingback-flanker. Occasionally he may be put in the backfield, providing the capability of running the three back offense. The fast and talented Z backs develop into fine pass receivers. Those with lower skill levels are journeyman receivers, and their blocking abilities can be used to a greater degree.

The X back plays the fullback position and sometimes the halfback spots (the halfback on the tight side is the halfback and the halfback on the split side is the quick halfback). The X back must be a good blocker. If he is an excellent runner the offense can be tailored to suit these talents. The best running back is the Y back, who will play at tailback, either halfback, or set out as a wing or slot in certain spread formations. If the Y back can be taught to be an effective blocker, you can take advantage of that ability. One or both running backs can be utilized as pass receivers if they have that ability.

If there is a great difference in the ability levels of one side of the line as opposed to the other, the right side and split side can be flopped, providing right and left formations. You can get the better blockers to either side of the field by flopping.

Signalling

Plays are sent in from the bench by signalling or using a substitute. In the huddle, the quarterback calls out the formation direction, the backfield set, motion (if used), the play word or number, the blocking pattern, and the snap number. This sounds complicated, but you will see in the following chapters how simply it can be done.

Spacing

Line spacing is illustrated in Diagram 3-1. There is a two-foot split from center to guard, and a three-foot split for the rest of the line. The holes are numbered so that odd holes are to the right and even holes to the left, as in Diagram 3-2. When left formations are used the odd and even holes are flopped. Ends split at 1 yard, 4 yards, or 10 yards. The Z back can be at a tight slot or wing, or flanked up to 14 yards.

DIAGRAM 3-1: Line Spacing (ends may vary)

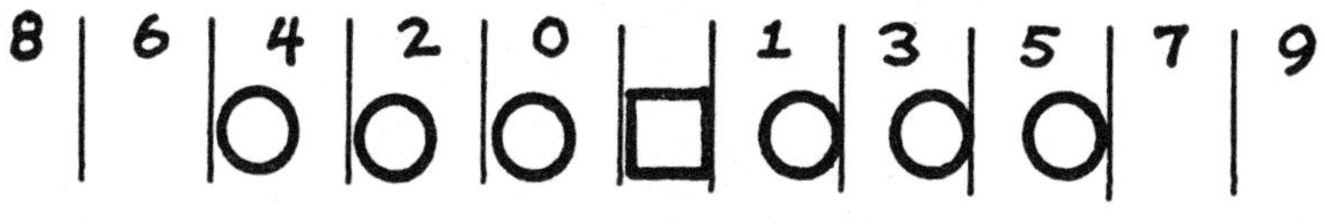

8 | 6 | 4 | 2 | 0 | 1 | 3 | 5 | 7 | 9

DIAGRAM 3-2: Hole Numbers

Blocking Rules

To simplify blocking rules, the defensive front is counted. Count anyone within 4 yards of the line of scrimmage. If the center strikes a defender in that 4 yard area by coming off the ball straight ahead, he is #0, as shown in Diagram 3-3. Count the other defenders inside out. If there is doubt about a defender being within 4 yards of the line of scrimmage, count him. Count stacks so that the closer defender has the lower number. Examples of numbering fronts are in Diagrams 3-4, 3-5, and 3-6. It may be necessary to change numbering sequence occasionally in order to meet specific situations.

It is critical that players count and point to the defenders at the line of scrimmage. The center finds and points to #0, the guards point to #1, the tackles to #2, and the ends to #3. The blockers may not be assigned to these men, but if they are counted off from inside out, it will reduce confusion regarding the number of each defender.

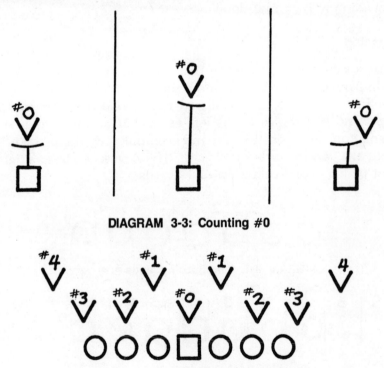

DIAGRAM 3-3: Counting #0

DIAGRAM 3-4: Counting Defensive Front

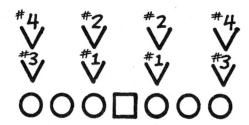

DIAGRAM 3-5: Counting Defensive Front

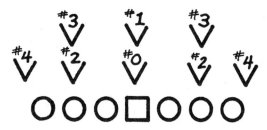

DIAGRAM 3-6: Counting Defensive Front

Definitions

The following definitions provide a system of communication:

1. *Odd*—Call made by center if #0 exists
2. *Even*—Call made by center when there is no #0
3. *Lineman*—A defender within four yards of the line who is in a stance with one or both hands on the ground
4. *Linebacker*—A defender within four yards of the line of scrimmage who is in an upright stance; an upright defender who is clearly on the line is treated as a lineman
5. *On*—A lineman positioned so that the blocker would strike him if he released perpendicular to the line of scrimmage
6. *Over*—A linebacker positioned so that the blocker would strike him if he released perpendicular to the line of scrimmage.
7. *Inside gap*—A lineman positioned between a blocker and the next offensive blocker to the inside

8. *Outside gap*—A lineman positioned between a blocker and the next blocker outside

9. *First*—First lineman from center out

10. *Second*—Second lineman from center out

11. *A, B, C, D,* etc.—Enumeration of defenders within four yards of the line of scrimmage from outside in

12. *Alpha, Bravo, Charlie, Delta,* etc.—Enumeration of linemen from outside in

chapter 4

Setting the Flexible Offense

The primary purpose for using multiple sets and formations is to align your offensive personnel in the best positions from which to carry out the desired play. If your preparation is good, multiple sets, formations, and motion are excellent ways to control the defensive schemes. If the defense has adjustment problems or is confused as a result of the multiple alignments, that is an additional bonus.

Formations

In the Modular structure formations are the alignments of the line and Z back. A *Right* or *East* call puts the tight side on the right, the split side on the left, and the Z back in the backfield. A *Left* or *West* call positions the tight side on the left of the center with the Z back in the backfield (Diagram 4-1). A *North* formation positions the Z back at a wing position with the line to the right (Diagram 4-2). The opposite call is *South*. A *Star* positions the Z back at a wing position on the left with the line to the right (Diagram 4-3), with its opposite designated *Port*. A *Gee* flanks the Z back ten yards outside the tight end's position (he will never align closer to the sideline than five yards), while the *Haw* is its reciprocal (Diagram 4-4). A *Pro* flanks the Z back to the left with the line right, while a *Con* is the opposite (Diagram 4-5).

End Spacing

There is a modifier which adjusts wing sets so that the end on that side is split 2 yards and the wing is slotted inside, as in *North-Dub, Star-Dub, South-Dub,* or *Port-Dub* (Diagram 4-6). Flank formations can be modified by using the word *Board* to indicate a width of 5 yards, as in *Gee-Board* (Diagram 4-7).

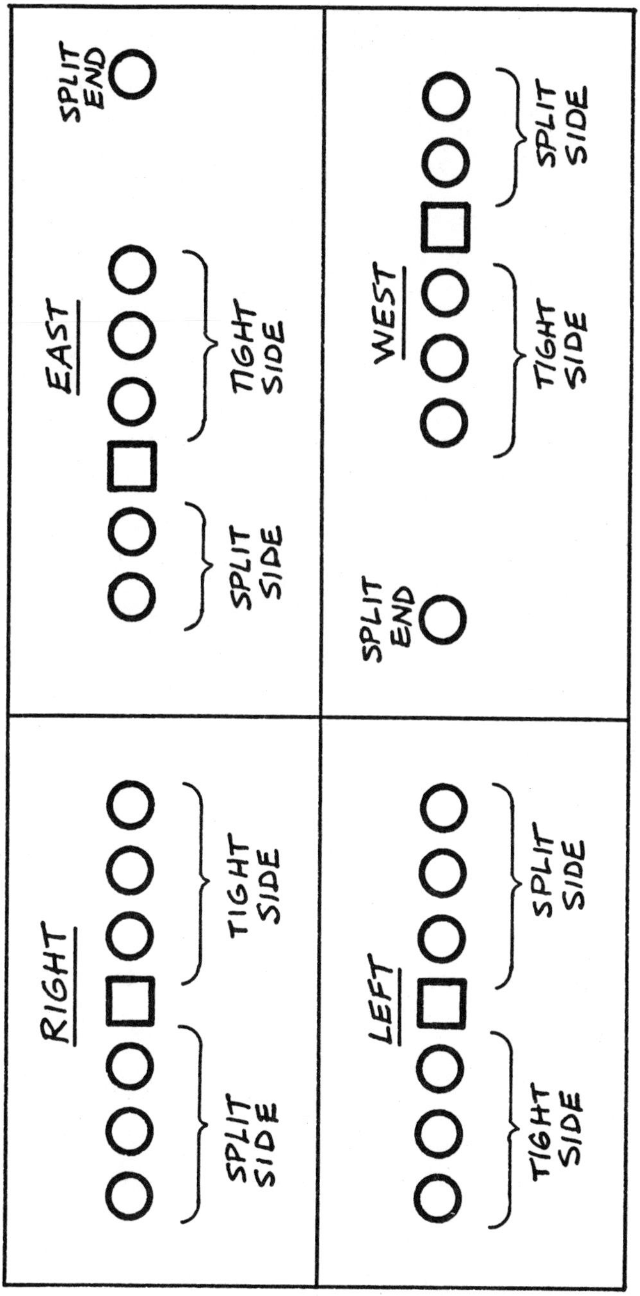
SPLIT END
EAST
TIGHT SIDE
SPLIT SIDE
WEST
SPLIT SIDE
TIGHT SIDE
SPLIT END
RIGHT
TIGHT SIDE
SPLIT SIDE
LEFT
SPLIT SIDE
TIGHT SIDE

DIAGRAM 4-1

DIAGRAM 4-2: *North (South* is opposite)

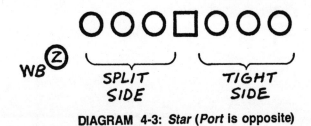

DIAGRAM 4-3: *Star (Port* is opposite)

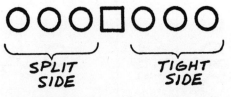

DIAGRAM 4-4: *Gee (Haw* is opposite)

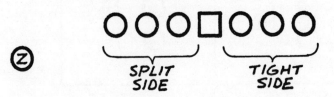

DIAGRAM 4-5: *Pro (Con* is opposite)

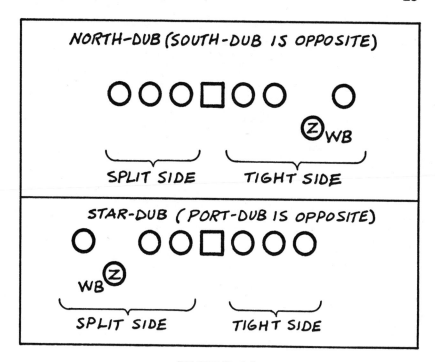

DIAGRAM 4-6

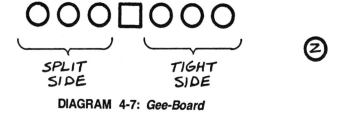

DIAGRAM 4-7: *Gee-Board*

The split end is widened by adding *Split* to the call, which positions him 10 yards outside his original alignment (Diagram 4-8). He never aligns closer to the sideline than 5 yards. *Pickle* positions him 4 yards from his original position (Diagram 4-9). If the split end is moved to the right in an end over, use the word *East*, which places him 10 yards outside the tight end. The opposite formation is a *West* (Diagram 4-10).

The tight end aligns 10 yards outside his tackle when he hears *String*, and 4 yards outside the tackle when he hears *Flex*.

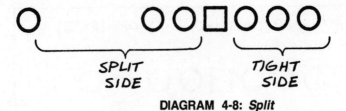

DIAGRAM 4-8: *Split*

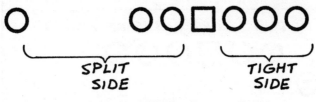

DIAGRAM 4-9: *Pickle*

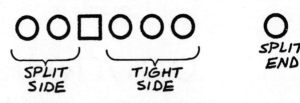

DIAGRAM 4-10: *East (West* is opposite)

A twins formation is created by using *Pro-Split* (the end splits 10 yards and the Z back positions 4 yards outside the end), or *Gee-String*. An end over twins is created by using *East-Gee* or *West-Haw*. The opposite of *Pro-Split* is *Con-Split*, while the opposite of *Gee-String* is *Haw-String*.

Back Sets

Use letters to align the backfield. The backfield sets are relative to the direction of alignment of the line. An *A* set aligns the Y back so that he splits the stance of the split tackle with his outside foot, putting him on the left side when the line is right, and on the right side when the line is left. This is known as the quick halfback position (Diagram 4-11). In the *A* set, the X back is in the fullback position.

The *B* set places the Y back splitting the stance of the tight tackle with his outside foot, and puts the X back in the fullback position (Diagram 4-12). In this set the Y back is in the halfback position.

The *C* set puts the Y back at the halfback spot and the X back at the quick halfback position (Diagram 4-13), while the *D* set aligns the X back at halfback and the Y back at quick halfback (Diagram 4-14).

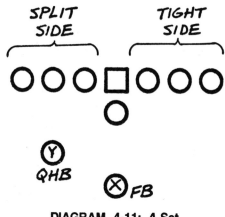

DIAGRAM 4-11: *A* Set

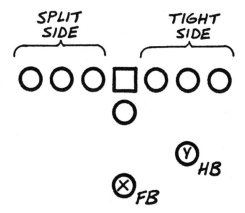

DIAGRAM 4-12: *B* Set

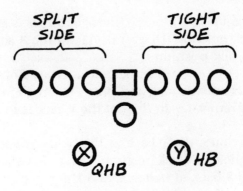

DIAGRAM 4-13: *C* Set

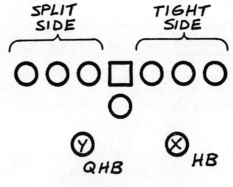

DIAGRAM 4-14: *D* Set

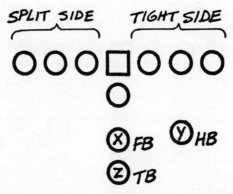

DIAGRAM 4-15: *I Right* (*I Left* is opposite)

The *I* places the X at fullback with the Y at tailback, aligned 5 1/2 yards to 8 yards deep, depending on the play called and his ability. The offensive fullback is about 4 yards off the ball, while the halfbacks are a shade less than that. The Z back is brought into the offensive backfield by using an *I Right, East, Quick-Right, Quick-East, I Left, West, Quick-Left,* or *Quick-West* call (Diagrams 4-15 through 4-18).

To call one back sets use the supplement *L,* which aligns the Y back on the split side in the wing position. Examples of such combinations are *L Gee-Split* (Diagram 4-19), *L Pro-Split* (Diagram 4-20), *L-D North-String* (Diagram 4-21). You can align two backs in an offset *I* or cockeye look by using sets such as *C-I* or *D-I* (Diagram 4-22), or can align in *A, B, C, D, C-I,* or *D-I Veer* by positioning the quick halfback or halfback directly behind the guard and 5 yards deep.

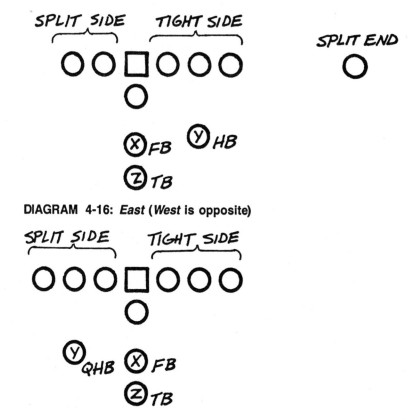

DIAGRAM 4-16: *East (West is opposite)*

DIAGRAM 4-17: *Quick-Right (Quick-Left is opposite)*

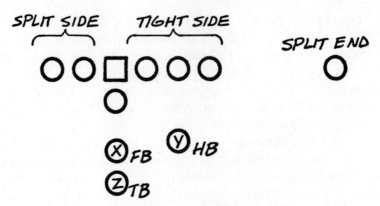

DIAGRAM 4-18: *Quick-East (Quick West is opposite)*

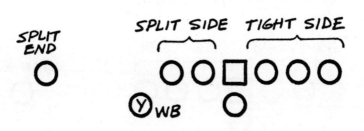

DIAGRAM 4-19: *L-Gee-Split*

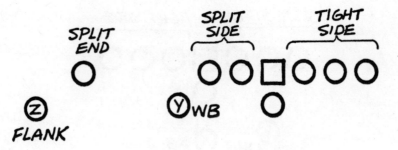

DIAGRAM 4-20: *L-Pro-Split*

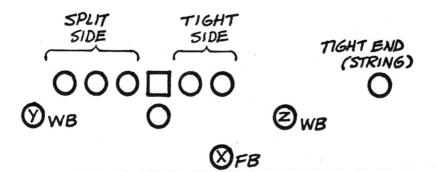

DIAGRAM 4-21: *L-D North-String*

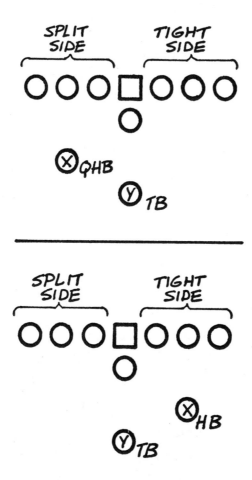

DIAGRAM 4-22: *C-I* or *D-I* Sets

Do not attempt to teach all sets or formations in a given year; use from 5 to 10 for each given week. The communications system allows the flexibility to tailor alignments year by year and game by game. When the offense develops unanticipated shortcomings or talents, methods can be modified to use the system to best advantage. You can adapt it to your needs and talents.

It is impossible to list all the possible combinations of sets, end placements, and formations, but here are some examples:

1. *I Gee-Split* (Diagram 4-23)
2. *A Star-Split-String* (Diagram 4-24)
3. *D-I Pro-Split-Flex* (Diagram 4-25)
4. *B North-East* (Diagram 4-26)

The system has enough flexibility to allow use of the formations which best accomplish your objectives.

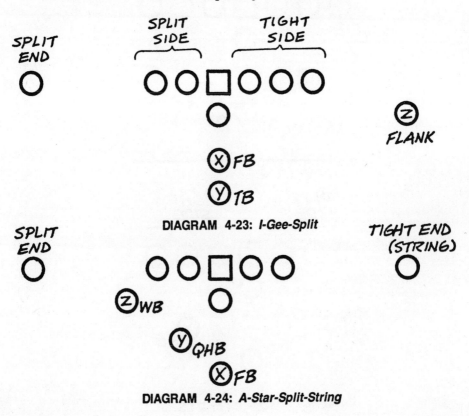

DIAGRAM 4-23: *I-Gee-Split*

DIAGRAM 4-24: *A-Star-Split-String*

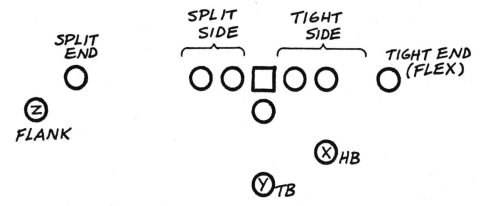

DIAGRAM 4-25: *D-I-Pro-Split-Flex*

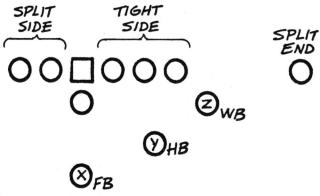

DIAGRAM 4-26: *B North-East*

Shifting

Shifting is as old as Stagg. Like other trends in football, it travels in cycles. Today, many coaches are shifting because "America's Team" does it. There is one very strong reason to shift: it enables the offense to get to the set or formation desired while giving the defense a very short time to read the formation. The defensive team must be prepared to defend the pre-shift or any intermediate shift, and then the final formation.

Usually the shifting base is an *I* set and a wing formation. It can be altered from week to week to any shifting base that is advantageous. To go to a *B Gee-Split*, shift to it from an *I North* on the "Ready" command from the quarterback; that puts the linemen in stances and moves personnel to the finish forma-

tion (Diagram 4-27). The split end is aligned in his finish formation for *East* or *West* formations, and it is not usual to shift sets
in which the Z back is a running back. With this shifting base,
an *I North* requires no shift. An *Opposite* call starts the Z back
in a wing position on the side away from the finish formation,
as in *A Gee-Split Opposite* (Diagram 4-28). To shift twice, call
Double Shift; the ends and Z back will make their shift on
"Ready," while X and Y will go from the shifting base to any set
they wish, shifting to the final set on the *Set* command.

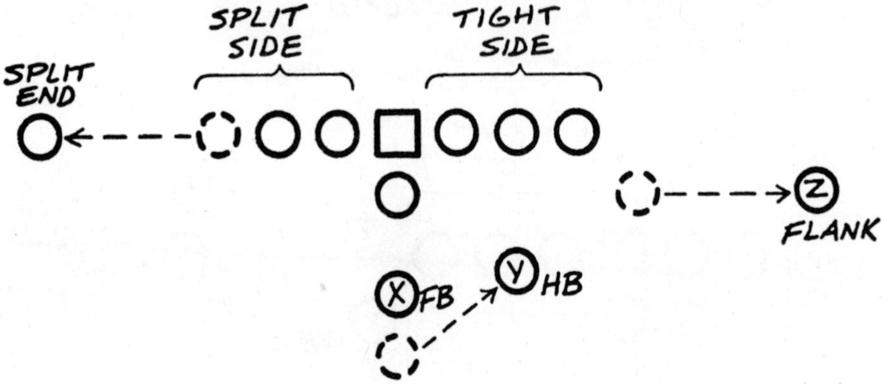

DIAGRAM 4-27: Shift from *I North* to *B-Gee-Split*

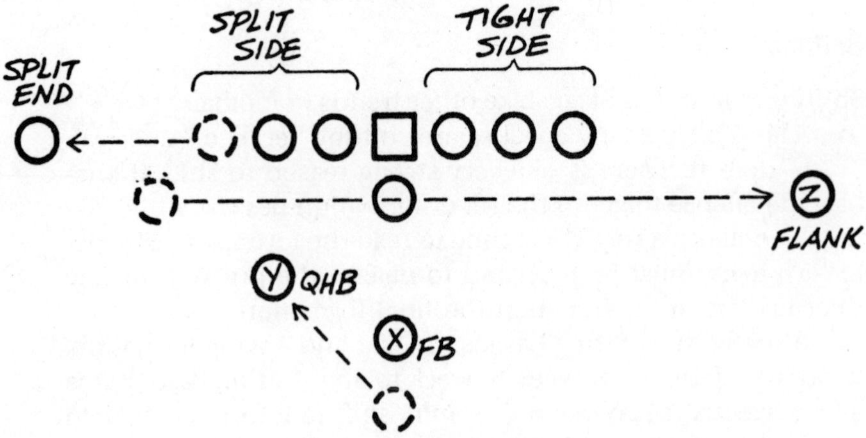

DIAGRAM 4-28: Shift to *A-Gee-Split* Opposite

There are times when shifting serves no purpose. If the defense does not adjust (psychologically or technically) to the strength of your formations, or if shifting causes the defense to move so as to destroy your desired reads of the defense, or if you are in the "two minute drill" and must expedite the plays, you will not want to shift. In these situations, use the *No Shift* call. You may decide not to shift the ends or Z back. You have the flexibility to do whatever you want when you want to do it in shifting. Usually the calls of *Opposite, No Shift, Double Shift,* and others are used early in the practice week. As the players learn how the shifting is done for a particular game plan, you can eliminate those words from the huddle call.

Motion

The use of motion in the offense enables you to change the formation up to the time of the snap. Used intelligently, it causes the defense to change coverage assignments, creates a distraction for linebackers and ends, and enables you to get your strength to the point of attack.

Motion is initiated with a foot signal by the quarterback, a look and nod at the motion back by the quarterback, or one count before the non-rhythmic snap signal. *Fly* brings the Z back toward the formation (Diagram 4-29), *Float* takes him away from the formation (Diagram 4-30), *Zip* takes him across the formation (Diagram 4-31), *Zap* starts him toward the formation to the position of the end, where he reverses and goes away from formation (Diagram 4-32).

X and Y can be given motion by the call of X or Y *Zig* or *Zag*, the *Zig* taking the back to the side of the play, and the *Zag* moving the back to the side opposite the play (Diagram 4-33).

DIAGRAM 4-29: *Fly* **Motion**

DIAGRAM 4-30: *Float* Motion

DIAGRAM 4-31: *Zip* Motion

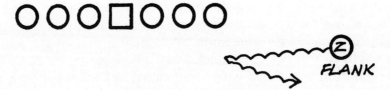

DIAGRAM 4-32: *Zap* Motion

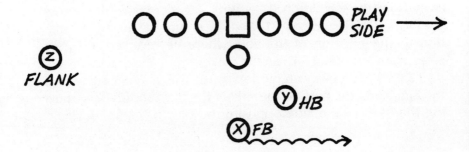

DIAGRAM 4-33: *X Zig* Motion

A Simple Audible System

A quarterback audible system must be simple. The most effective tool is to teach the quarterback in the classroom and on the field how to read the defense, calling out a code word to change the huddle call to the mirror play on the other side of the line. To avoid shifting, do this from formations with both ends tight and an *I, C,* or *D* set.

Occasionally a run and a pass are called from the same formation in the huddle, with the quarterback calling the play according to his read by using a live color at the line of scrimmage. Experiments have been done with other systems of audibles, but the listed methods were found most effective.

With methods to implement the offense in place, you can break the huddle and line up properly. The question now is whom to block.

The most challenging task for a football coach is teaching blocking assignments. The problem is compounded by changing defensive alignments, fronts that move on the snap of the football, and players well coached in defensive techniques and employed in superbly conceived defensive team play. The coach who formulates blocking assignments for a running play must consider the following elements: (1) The speed with which the play hits the line of scrimmage (2) the kind of play to be run in relation to fakes, backfield flow, etc. (3) the personnel on the offensive line and (4) defensive keys. As the season progresses, the coach can alter assignments to fit the defense he will see in a given week and the opponents' personnel.

A word is used to designate blocking patterns for the line and the blocking back. When combined with the direction of the run (odd or even side), this communicates his assignment to the offensive lineman. It is remarkable how few different assignments there are for each lineman. Many of the modules are similar and are grouped so that some of the modules have submodules.

Modules for All Line Positions

All the modules for each line position and the blocking back are listed on a chart (Diagram 5-1). Various play actions can be combined with different modules, giving a tremendous variety of ways to execute the offense. Not every action is combined with every blocking pattern because they do not all fit, but it is amazing how many different combinations are available.

Modules	Front E	Front T	Front G	C	Back G	Back T	Back E	Blocking Back
Base	Drive #3	Drive #2	Drive #1	Drive #0	Seal	Drive #2	Cross-field	None
Straight	Drive #3	Drive #2	Drive #1	Drive #0	Drive #1	Drive #2	Cross-field	None
Counter	Counter #3	Counter #2	Counter #1	Counter #0; none-read frnt blitz; block backside	Drive #1	Drive #2	Drive #3	None
Power	Odd-Dr#2 Even-Drive #3	Odd-Post #2; Even-Drive #2	Drive #1	Drive #0	Seal	Drive #2	Cross-field	FB-Odd-Drive #3 Even-Drive #4
Kick	Odd-Dr#2 Even-Drive #3	Odd-Post #2; Even-Drive #3	Drive #1	Drive #0	Seal	Drive #2	Cross-field	HB-Odd-Drive #3 Even-Drive #4
"O"	Odd-Dr#2 Even-Drive #3	Odd-Post #2; Even-Drive #2	Drive #1	Drive #0	Odd-Trap #3; Even-Trap #4	Seal	Cross-field	None
Arc	Release-Block force	Drive #2	Drive #1	Drive #0	Seal	Drive #2	Cross-field	None

DIAGRAM 5-1: Run Blocking Assignment Chart

(continued)

39

Modules	Front E	Front T	Front G	O	Back G	Back T	Back E	Blocking Back
Sweep	Climb #3	Drive #2	Pull, lead for LB	Lineman on; #1 backside	Pull, lead thru end	Seal	Cross-field	FB-drive inside leg of T
Broom	Climb #3	Inside gap; #1	Pull, lead for LB	Lineman on; #1 backside	Pull, lead thru end	Seal	Cross-field	HB-drive outside leg of T
Toss	Drive #3	Pull and lead	Drive #1	Drive #0	Seal	Cross-field	Cross-field	None
Trap	Lead inside #3	LB over or inside	Drive #0; LB inside	Post lineman on; #1 backside	Trap 1st lineman past C	Seal	Cross-field	None
Tackle Trap	Lead inside #3	LB over or inside	Drive #0; LB inside	Post lineman on; #1 backside	Post lineman on; backside gap; over	Trap 1st lineman past C	Inside gap, on, over	None
Wish	Release-Block force	Odd-Drive #1 Even-Drive #2	Odd-Post #1 Even-Drive #1	Drive #0	Trap lineman on or outside T's block	Drive #2	Cross-field	None
Blast	Drive #3	Drive #2	Drive #1	Drive #0	Seal	Drive #2	Cross-field	FB-Lead thru hole
Wham	Drive #3	Drive #2	Drive #1	Drive #0	Seal	Drive #2	Cross-field	FB-Lead thru hole

Lead	Inside to LB	Drive #2	Drive #1	Drive #0	Seal	Drive #2	Cross-field	HB-Drive #3
Wedge	Wedge	Wedge	Wedge	Wedge	Wedge	Wedge	Wedge	Wedge
Double	Drive #3	Drive #2	Drive #0 if line-man; Post #1	Post #0 if lineman drive #1 backside	Seal	Drive #2	Cross-field	None
Hinge	Drive #3	Drive #2	Drive #1	Lineman on; drive #1 backside	Hitch; drive LB over or inside playside G	Drive #2	Drive #3	None
Draw	Stalk	Draw #2	Draw #1	Draw #0	Draw #1	Draw #2	Stalk	None
Pin	Lead in-side #3	Drive #2	Drive #0 if line-man; if not, drive #1	Drive thru out-side knee of #0 to #1 back-side	Trap LB over C, playside G, back-side G	Seal	Cross-field	None
Tackle Pin	Lead in-side #3	Drive #2	Drive #0 if line-man; if not, drive #1	Drive thru out-side knee of #0 to #1 back-side	Post lineman on; back-side gap; over	Trap LB over C, playside G, back-side G	Inside gap, on, over	None

DIAGRAM 5-1: Run Blocking Assignment Chart (cont.)

Base and Sub-Modules

The *Base* (Diagram 5-2) module directs each lineman on the playside to execute a drive block on his number, targeting the block so that a seam will be created at the desired hole. For the "3" hole, the tight guard attacks the outside hip or armpit of #1 and the tight tackle attacks the inside hip or armpit of #2. The center executes his #0 rule, with the backside guard executing a seal, the backside tackle driving #2 (if #2 is not threatening, he will go crossfield), and the backside end going crossfield. There is no blocking back on *Base*. The purpose is to knock the defense off the ball at the point of attack, forming a bubble in the defensive front; the good running back will find a crack.

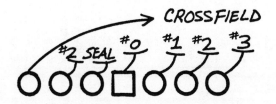

DIAGRAM 5-2: *Base* **(odd side)**

A sub-module of the *Base* is *Straight* (Diagram 5-3), in which all the linemen attack their numbers. There is no blocking back. The *Straight* is an excellent scheme to encourage cutback running, taking advantage of the soft spots in the defense. When combined with tailback plays or delayed plays, it permits the back to read the softness in the defensive front.

DIAGRAM 5-3: *Straight*

Another sub-module of the *Base* is *Counter* (Diagram 5-4), which is used for delayed or cutback plays, but is employed most frequently for misdirection plays. The fake side (backside) makes drive blocks on the inside of their defenders, while the counter side (play side) makes higher and somewhat softer blocks on their defenders, steering them the way they allow themselves to be taken. The counter block lies somewhere between the drive block and the draw block, probably a little closer to the drive block. If the defender is a lineman inside the blocker, the counter block changes to a drive block. In this scheme, the center counter blocks #0; if there is no #0 he steps to the counter side (playside) and takes a blitz if it comes; if he does not spot that blitz on the first step, he steps back to the backside and takes that blitz or blocks the first linebacker to his outside.

DIAGRAM 5-4: *Counter*

Power and Sub-Modules

The *Power* module is an off-tackle double team and trap by the lead back (Diagram 5-5). The rules are written so that the double team is against an odd front; if the defense fits the definition of an even front, single block and kick out #4 instead of #3; if there is a wing against the even front, double with the end and wing. The fullback is always the blocking back in this scheme. He takes two steps straight at the hips of the playside guard by leading with the playside foot, planting on the second step, then targeting his route to the inside armpit of the defender. The fullback must be prepared to go up into the line to dig out the defender if necessary. The runner reads the block of the fullback.

The *Kick* (Diagram 5-6) is a sub-module of *Power* which provides the same scheme, except the playside halfback takes a step forward with the outside foot, then steps and plants with the inside foot, and runs at the inside armpit of his defender. He must be prepared to go up into the line to dig out the de-

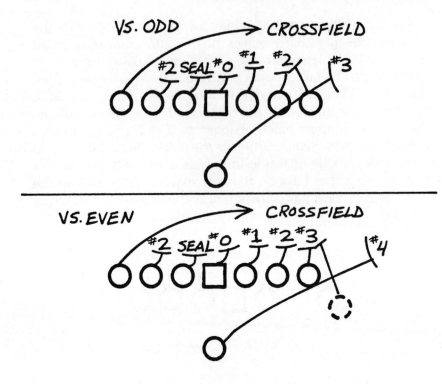

DIAGRAM 5-5: *Power* (odd side)

fender if necessary. Depending on the defensive front, the defender to be blocked by the back will be #3 or #4.

The *0* (Diagram 5-7) is another sub-module of *Power*. There is no blocking back, so the backside guard pulls and traps #3 on odd, #4 on even. The backside tackle seals because of the pulling guard. The *0* is frequently used when there is a fake into the middle of the line.

The *Arc* (Diagram 5-8) is a version of the *Power* in which the playside end takes a flat path to the outside, plants on the third step, then turns upfield. He blocks the defender who is coming up and forcing the play. The other linemen block the same as *Base*, and there is no lead back. *Arc* is a good option play scheme, and is used with run to daylight plays, sometimes in combination with a block by a back. With defensive ends who are very concerned with holding up the end's release into pass coverage, the *Arc* can be an effective tool.

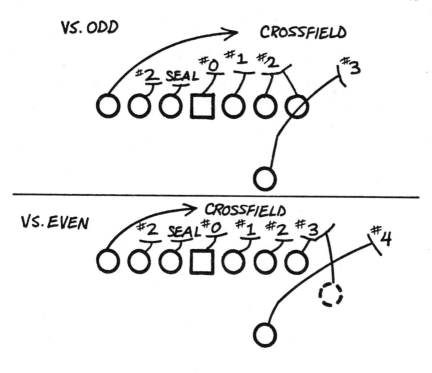

DIAGRAM 5-6: *Kick* (odd side)

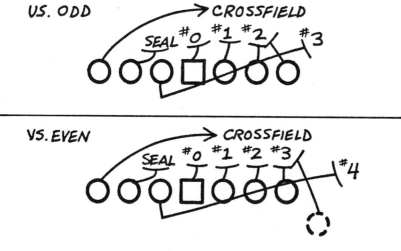

DIAGRAM 5-7: *0* (odd side)

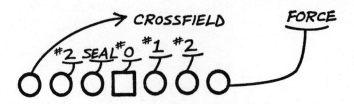

DIAGRAM 5-8: *Arc* **(odd side)**

The *Sweep*

The *Sweep* (Diagram 5-9) is designed to create a soft spot in the defensive front, permitting the running back to find a seam and accelerate through it. The playside end executes a climb block on #3. The climb block is similar to the counter block; the blocker makes contact at the inside armpit of the defender, stays with his man and runs with him to the sideline; he does not give up the inside. The fullback fills hard by squaring up shoulders at the inside leg of the playside tackle's initial alignment. The playside guard pulls and passes just in front of the fullback, moving parallel to the line of scrimmage. If the playside end is making his block on the line or to the inside, the lead guard turns upfield just outside the end's block and gets across the line of scrimmage to a depth of about 3 yards, then turns to the inside and walls off the linebacker's pursuit to the inside. If the end is riding #3 outside and wide, the frontside guard gets inside the end's block and turn upfield. The backside guard pulls and takes a flat course, keying his playside guard, running just behind him and blocking the first defender to show. There is a seal by the backside tackle and the end is coming crossfield. Generally this play will not develop as a wide play; the running back finds the soft spot and cuts through it; the spot is usually the off tackle hole. This is actually an old single wing play.

The *Broom*

The *Broom* (Diagram 5-10) is a variation of the *Sweep*, in which the playside halfback drives over the outside leg of the playside tackle. The playside tackle blocks his inside gap as first priority, then blocks #1 as his next priority. Apart from this, *Broom* is

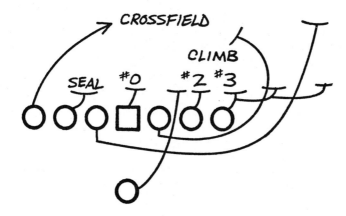

DIAGRAM 5-9: *Sweep* (odd side)

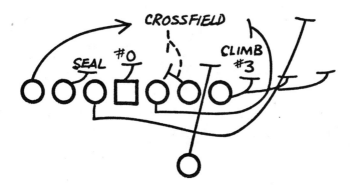

DIAGRAM 5-10: *Broom* (odd side)

the same kind of play as the *Sweep*. This is the classic Green Bay *Sweep* principle. A coaching point to remember is that the playside guard must get some depth on *Broom*, to allow the playside halfback to get to the line before the guard passes that point.

The *Toss*

The *Toss* (Diagram 5-11) is a way to get wide very quickly. It uses a drive block by the playside end (he actually aims a bit to the outside of the defender's hip, making it a hook block) and a quick pull by the playside tackle, who drives any penetrator who crosses the line of scrimmage; if there is no penetrator, the tackle turns and leads upfield. Both the backside tackle and backside guard go crossfield on this scheme. *Toss* is excellent for the quick pitch play, and sometimes works well for a tailback pitch or quick running play to the outside by the backside halfback.

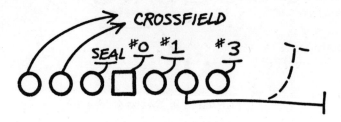

DIAGRAM 5-11: *Toss* (odd side)

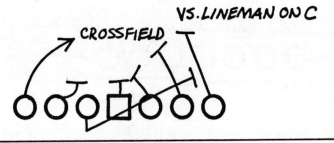

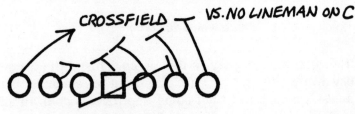

DIAGRAM 5-12: *Trap* (odd side)

The *Trap* and Sub-Modules

The *Trap* (Diagram 5-12) is a time-honored blocking scheme. It is a fine way to create openings in the defensive front without overpowering the defenders, making use of the defensive team's reactions or movements in order to make the hole. It enables blockers to get off the line of scrimmage and block linebackers and secondary personnel. The trap technique by the backside guard must be perfected by insisting that he take a short step with his near foot at the defender to be trapped, then proceed on an inside-out path to the inside armpit of that defender. If the defender closes the play, the blocker can turn his shoulders upfield and drive him off the ball. In any other situation the trapper can adjust his path, or the defender has taken himself out of the play. If there is a defensive lineman on the center, there is a double team block by the center and the playside guard, while other fronts involve angle blocks by the offensive line.

The *Tackle Trap* (Diagram 5-13) is a trap scheme in which there is better timing and a better blocking set-up for delayed plays. It is especially good for slow hitting misdirection plays, taking away the easy key for 5-2 linebackers. There is a double team against a defensive lineman who is on the center or against a defender on the nose of the backside guard. The tackle trap is preferred to the guard trap, but the guard trap is needed for the quick trap plays. The rules for traps can get quite complicated if you try to block every possible front. Con-

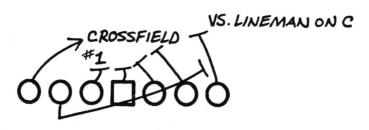

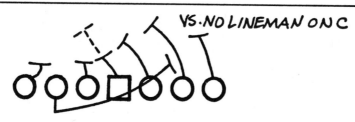

DIAGRAM 5-13: *Tackle Trap* (odd side)

sequently a blocking call is often built into the game plan, in which the trap will be called off against a front we are not prepared to trap. You might substitute *Straight, Counter, Pin,* or *Tackle Pin* (trapping linebackers).

The *Wish* (Diagram 5-14) is a version of the *Trap* which is frequently tied in with a *Trap* option play. If it is an even look, trap one hole wider for *Wish*. The *Trap* technique is combined with an arc technique by the playside end. Other kinds of backfield movements can be used for the *Wish* scheme, particularly in situations where the opposing end or outside linebacker jumps on the end when he arcs.

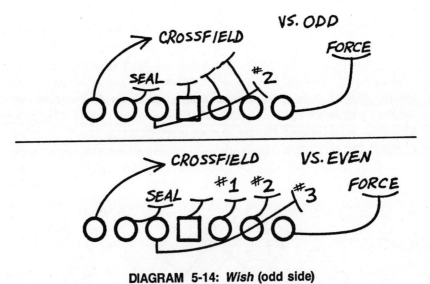

DIAGRAM 5-14: *Wish* **(odd side)**

The *Blast* and Sub-Modules

The *Blast* (Diagram 5-15) is the same as *Base* for the line except the fullback drives to the outside of the block of the hole lineman. It is an excellent play for tailback runs or backside halfback runs. The fullback's alignment can be cheated to a tighter position and he can lead the dive play with his block.

The *Wham* (Diagram 5-16) is the same as *Base* for the line but the playside halfback leads through the hole. It is an excel-

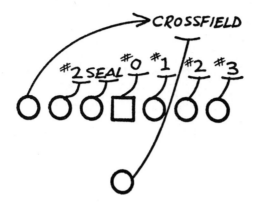

DIAGRAM 5-15: *Blast* (at hole #3)

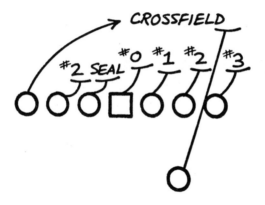

DIAGRAM 5-16: *Wham* (at #5 hole)

lent fullback run scheme and is used occasionally for tailback plays. You can cheat the halfback's realignment tighter and lead fullback plays with him. *Wham* is a sub-module of *Blast*.

Another sub-module of *Blast* is *Lead* (Diagram 5-17). The line drive blocks while the playside halfback drives #3 by running a straight line path to his inside armpit. If the playside end is tight, he drives the first linebacker to his inside. If the playside end is split, he stalks his defender. This is an excellent play into a split end, with the fullback carrying the ball and reading the soft spot.

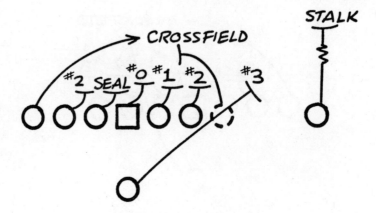

DIAGRAM 5-17: *Lead* **(odd side)**

The *Wedge*

The *Wedge* (Diagram 5-18) assigns each lineman to run through the armpit of the next offensive lineman to his inside, with the center designated the apex of the wedge. The center attacks a down lineman on him or to either gap; if there is none the tight guard is the apex and attacks the down lineman on him; if none, the center is again the apex and attacks the closest linebacker to his tight side. The *Wedge* is a scheme which lends itself to quick hitting halfback or fullback plays, particularly those in which a short yardage or goal line defense is faced. It is also excellent for quarterback sneaks. If the halfbacks are in position, each of them will drive over the outside leg of the tackle on his side to seal the wedge.

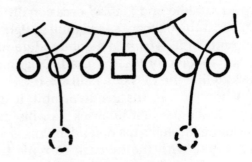

DIAGRAM 5-18: *Wedge*

The *Double*

The *Double* (Diagram 5-19) uses a double team on the lineman on the center; if another front, double #1 to the tight side. The rest of the line blocks *Base*. This scheme is sometimes used in combination with a *Blast* or a *Wham*. The effectiveness of the double team-isolation play has been reduced in modern football because of the linebacker's proficiency in reading a lineman's down block, thus closing the play.

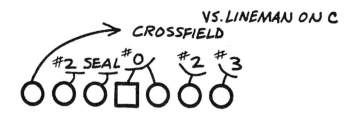

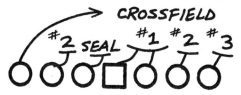

DIAGRAM 5-19: *Double* (odd side)

The *Hinge*

The *Hinge* (Diagram 5-20) directs the backside guard to hitch and come around the center's block. This assignment is to drive the linebacker from the tight guard to the backside. The center blocks on or #1 to the backside. It is a good scheme for the running back to cut back and read the backside pursuit.

The *Draw*

The *Draw* (Diagram 5-21) means that the ends come off the line of scrimmage as for a pass. When their defenders slow down to react back for the run, the ends come under control and exe-

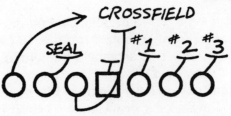

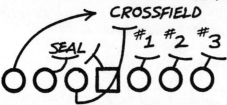

DIAGRAM 5-20: *Hinge (odd side)*

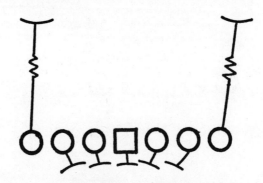

DIAGRAM 5-21: *Draw*

cute the stalk block. The interior line sets up to pass block; if the defender on an offensive lineman penetrates, the blocker steers him to the outside deep or drives him hard inside. If the offensive lineman is not covered or his position is not rushed, he sets as if to pass block for two counts, then leads the play upfield. True draw plays work well with this scheme, but there are many slow misdirection plays that also get excellent results.

Combination Plays

Combinations of the various schemes are made by using calls such as *Double Wham* (Diagram 5-22), *Kick Blast* (Diagram 5-23), or *Double Straight* (Diagram 5-24). There are many other possibilities. When a combination call is made, the first word will signify the line assignments and the second word will indicate the backfield assignments.

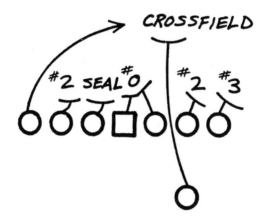

DIAGRAM 5-22: *Double Wham* **(odd side)**

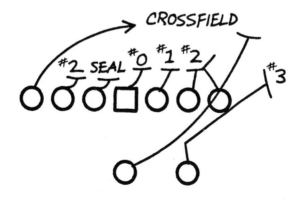

DIAGRAM 5-23: *Kick-Blast* **(odd side)**

DIAGRAM 5-24: *Double Straight* (odd side)

Importance of Line Calls

Because of the many defensive fronts, line calls are necessary. These are in addition to the schemes which are called in the huddle. The game plan is sometimes designed so in certain situations the entire scheme can be changed at the line of scrimmage. You can also have a system of quarterback audibles available. Despite these possibilities, line calls are necessary.

Special Situations

When an offensive lineman is blocking a linebacker for a running play at least one hole wider than his position (this is a defensive bubble), he steps to his outside with the outside foot. The step must be flat and down the line; if the defensive lineman to his outside is moving to the inside, the blocker drive blocks this defender (Diagram 5-25), while the blocker to the

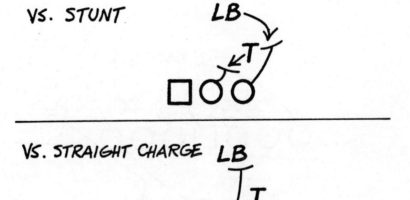

DIAGRAM 5-25: *Scoop* Maneuver

outside runs through on the linebacker. If the defensive lineman is not moving to the inside, the inside blocker turns upfield and blocks the linebacker; the outside blocker makes the block on the lineman as he is targeting through the outside hip. This maneuver is called a *Scoop*.

When the defense is aligned shaded, overshifted, with a stack or near stack, you may want to call a *Hit and Run* and have the outside blocker drive for the armpit of the down lineman to his inside, bounce and drive the linebacker, while the inside lineman drives through the outside hip of the down lineman (Diagram 5-26).

In the *Loop* (Diagram 5-27), the inside lineman makes a hitch step and eyeballs the linebacker; if the linebacker is coming the blocker attacks him; if not, he pulls around the offensive lineman to his outside and attacks the linebacker. He keeps his eyes on the linebacker throughout this maneuver.

Sometimes it is necessary for two offensive linemen to exchange assignments. You can do this by using the *Combo* call illustrated in Diagram 5-28.

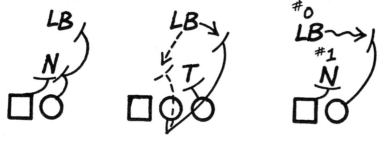

DIAGRAM 5-26:
Hit and Run

DIAGRAM 5-27: *Loop*

DIAGRAM 5-28:
Combo Call

The backside seal of the guard takes care of stunts on the backside if the center steps properly to the playside (Diagram 5-29). If defenders are targeted correctly and the defender moves across the face of a blocker, he will block the next defender outside, with the inside blocker taking the defender moving to the inside. This is actually zone blocking, so the stunting defense should be no problem.

If you want to block only the defenders on the line of scrimmage and not count the linebackers, a *Line* call is made,

VS. ANGLE
    FRONTSIDE

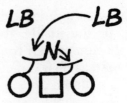

VS. ANGLE
    BACKSIDE

DIAGRAM 5-29: Zone Blocking Backside

assigning the guard, tackle, and end to the first, second, and third defenders on the line of scrimmage.

If a *Backer* call is made, the guard and tackle block the first and second men on the line of scrimmage, and the end blocks the linebacker over him or to the inside.

Wingback and Flanker Assignments

The wingbacks and flankers have simple blocking assignments. On the playside, the flanker stalks the defender covering him; his intention is to shield the defender from the ball carrier. The wing on the playside drives #4, running at him under control, accelerating through the target. The backside wingback and the flanker block crossfield.

6

Cut and Run: The Flexible 50 Series

$\mathbf{T}$he flow pattern of the 50 Series is shown in Diagram 6-1. It gives the "backbone" play of the *I*, the tailback sweep, a fullback off-tackle play, and a nice counter. We have illustrated all possible backfield positions and their routes in the flow diagram. If a blocking scheme is called in which a particular back has a blocking assignment, the blocking call takes precedence over the flow pattern.

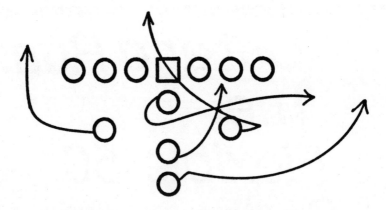

DIAGRAM 6-1: Flow Pattern—50 Series (odd side)

The Good Tailback and the *57 Sweep*

If you have a running back with ability to read blocks and cut (and who can catch the pitch), give this tailback sweep a lot of work. The good tailbacks get better and better as they get the feel of the play. It is an excellent short gainer and it will also get some long gains. The idea on the *57 Sweep* (Diagram 6-2) is to stretch the defensive front, emphasizing the climb block by the end. At some point the defense develops a seam and the good tailback accelerates through that opening; he has good interference in front of him.

To initiate the *57*, the quarterback puts weight on the tight side foot, reverse pivots, and makes a two hand pitch to the

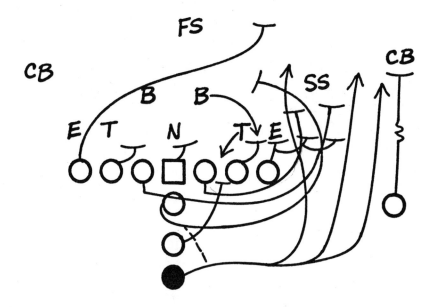

DIAGRAM 6-2: *I Gee, 57 Sweep vs. 5-2 Slant*

tailback. The pitch should be firm but not too hard, aimed at the numerals of the back. After the pitch, the quarterback gives a little ground and leads the play around the tight end's original position. He turns upfield to a depth of 5 yards and blocks to the inside. The tailback aligns from 7 to 7 1/2 yards deep. On the snap, the tailback takes a step with his playside foot directed at the inside foot of the tight end, then works parallel to the line of scrimmage. When he catches the pitch, he tucks in the ball securely, reads the cracks in the defense, and takes his daylight as soon as he recognizes it. On *Sweep*, the fullback drives over the inside leg of the tackle and squares up his shoulders, blocking the defender who shows up in that area. The fullback and playside tackle are responsible to zone block, and should limit penetration in that area. The guards pull and run routes which get them upfield in good lead blocking positions.

Other 50 Series Plays

If *57 Straight* is run the guards do not pull, and you take the defense off the ball. The *59 Toss* or *Blast* is designed to get wide with the tailback as soon as possible. On the split side, *56 or 58* from the various blocking modules are run.

Use *55* as an excellent way to attack the off-tackle hole. It can be run as *Base* with a tailback in the *I,* which lends some deception (looks like the *57* or *59*), or you can run it with a half-back employed in the blocking scheme. The quarterback reverse pivots, makes his first step at 6 o'clock (presuming he faces 12 o'clock when under the center), makes the second step at 4 o'clock, then extends the ball to the far elbow of the full-back. The quarterback bellies upfield after the handoff and runs to the sideline, as in his flow pattern for the 50 Series. The fullback steps for the outside leg of the tackle, rolls his shoulders to a parallel position, reads the blocks, and runs through the daylight. This is an excellent play from *Wham* when a half-back is in position (Diagram 6-3). It is very good from *Kick* or into a split end as *54 Lead* (Diagram 6-4). Success has been achieved with the fullback reading a jam at the hole and taking the play outside.

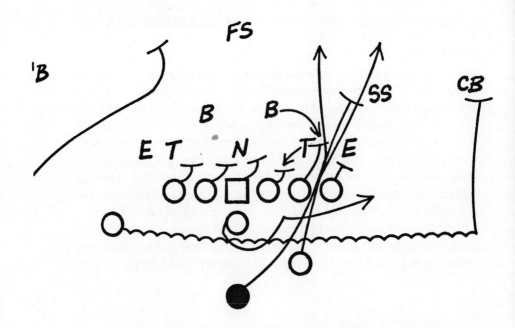

DIAGRAM 6-3: *B-Star-Split-Zip, 55 Wham vs. 5-2 Slant*

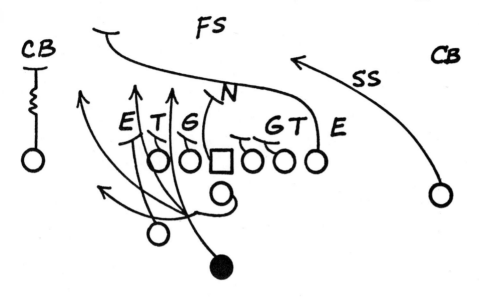

DIAGRAM 6-4: *A-Gee-Split 54 Lead* **vs.** *6-1*

An excellent misdirection for the 50 Series is the *50* or *51* play. The *50 Tackle Trap* can be devastating (Diagram 6-5) when it catches the defense overpursuing. Stick with this play; it can be a long gainer. When the offensive tackle blocks to his inside, the modern defensive tackle closes hard; when the guard blocks down on the nose guard, the *52* linebacker steps up. These maneuvers make the trap difficult; if that is the case, try the *50 Tackle Pin* (Diagram 6-6) in which the linebacker is trapped.

In the *50*, the halfback steps with the outside foot parallel to the line, plants and runs a route for the far leg of the center. He makes the plant step deliberately, and gets the inside elbow up to accept the handoff from the quarterback. He runs under control until he sees the daylight develop, at which point he accelerates. The quarterback reverse pivots and steps at 6 o'clock, then steps directly at the lineup position of the halfback, extends and looks the ball into the halfback's pocket, fading deep into the backfield after the handoff. This play is best executed with a fullback in position, because there is a fake and a fill. When it serves your purpose, execute the play from other

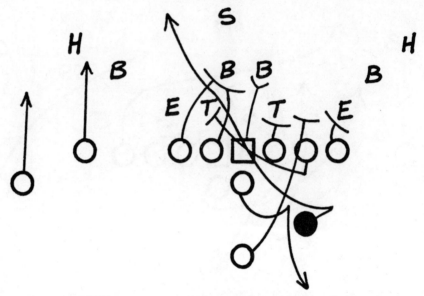

DIAGRAM 6-5: *B Pro-Split, 50 Tackle Trap* vs. 4-4

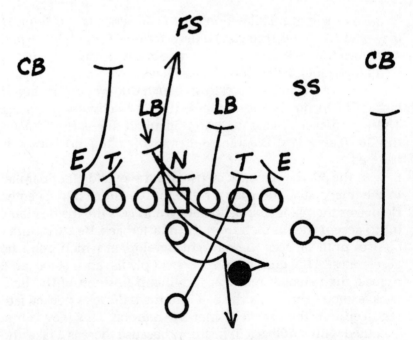

DIAGRAM 6-6: *B-North-Float, 50 Tackle Pin* vs. 5-2

sets. It is also a good play from a *Straight, Counter,* or *Draw.* If you want to run the play with draw blocking and include the ends in that blocking, make a *Sketch* call for the module.

The *51* play is a reciprocal of the *50.* Use the pitch to the tailback from the *I* if you have a fine running back. He does not need to be a speed merchant for the concept to be effective. The good back will stretch the defense and find a soft spot to accelerate through. The *57* or *56* with modules in which one or both guards pull are excellent against reading and flat pursuit defenses. If you have good speed, use the *59* or *58* combined with *Toss* or *Blast* modules, particularly if you are working against a defensive contain man who is a trifle slow. If your wide plays from the 50 Series cause the defense to drive the contain man deep across the line on the snap, make use of the *55* or *54* with the *Kick* or *Wham* modules. Take advantage of overpursuit, and miskey the defense by using the *50* or *51* plays.

chapter 7

Single Wing Reborn: The Flexible 60 Series

The tailback series from the *I* sets (Diagram 7-1) is a throwback to the single wing. The tailback receives the handoff deep in the backfield, reads the reactions of the defense, and accelerates through the daylight. This offensive pattern creates its own counter plays; the defense cannot afford to overpursue. The good tailback seems to get better each time he carries the ball; he gets the feel of the play as the game progresses. He may gain short yardage for many consecutive carries, then suddenly burst for a long gain.

The *65 Power*

The *65 Power* (Diagram 7-2) is a tried and true tailback off-tackle, with a double team by the end and tackle, and a kick-out block by the fullback. If the center calls an even defense, single block the numbers and the fullback kicks out the #4 man. The quarterback reverse pivots and puts his left foot at 6 o'clock, then crosses over with a long step at 4 o'clock. He makes this step as deep as possible so he can get the ball to the tailback deep in the backfield. On the second step the quarterback extends the ball with the left hand. He is aiming for the outside hip of the fullback and he looks the ball into the pocket. This enables him to make the necessary minute adjustments in the execution of the handoff. The quarterback takes three more deep steps, making the fifth step with his right foot pointed directly toward the sideline. This maneuver will start him on a path upfield in which he turns his shoulders and fakes a spring-out pass, checking the reactions of the defense.

The tailback takes a lead step with his right foot at a slight angle upfield from the sideline. His second step is at the outside leg of the tackle. He receives the ball on his second step. The tailback's responsibility on the exchange is to read the defense, step properly, and make a good pocket. Otherwise, the quarterback is responsible for getting the ball to him. The tailback breaks anywhere he sees the daylight, although he should expect it to be at the designated point of attack.

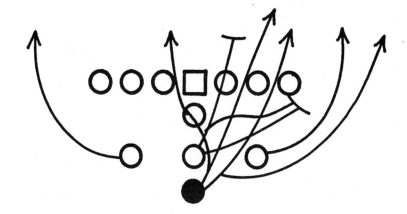

DIAGRAM 7-1: 60 Series—Flow Diagram—odd side

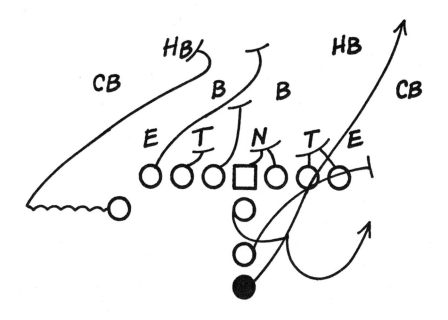

DIAGRAM 7-2: I Star Float, 65 Power vs. 5-2 Gap Stack

Double Team and Kick-Out Blocking

The effectiveness of double team and kick-out blocking has been minimized recently. The defender who is aligned on the end closes when his end blocks down and linebackers get quick pursuit, reducing the value of *65 Power*. Recently *65 Blast* has been used with better results. The fullback leads through the #5 hole and the tailback runs for the opening. The *64* plays are reciprocals for the *65* plays.

A *65* Combination

A combination or variation of *65 Power* and *Blast* is *65 0 Blast*. The fullback leads through the hole along with the end-tackle double team, but with a kick-out block by the backside guard, who traps #3 on odd, or #4 on even. There are many other variations of the *65* play. It is bread and butter. Execute it well, be creative with the blocking schemes when necessary, and it will pay dividends.

The *65 Keep*

A nice sequential take-off for *65* is the *65 Keep*. The quarterback makes his first two steps as in *65*, extends his left hand into the pocket of the faking tailback while holding the ball with his right hand against his outside hip, then flattens out his third step to the sideline and turns upfield. The fullback runs a path directly for a point 2 yards outside the tight end. The quarterback positions himself so he is a yard outside and a yard behind the fullback. If a defender crosses the projected arc of the ball carrier, the fullback blocks him to the outside by running through the inside armpit; otherwise the fullback turns upfield and leads the quarterback to the goal line (Diagram 7-3). An excellent coaching point for the quarterback is the importance of the eyes in faking to the tailback. If he looks at the tailback's pocket as he extends the open hand, and continues to look at the tailback one step after the fake, he will fool the defense. This is a fine play for the quarterback with running ability. Run the *65 Power Keep* (the *Keep* tells the fullback that he carries out that maneuver rather than the blocking scheme that is called) and *65 Blast Keep*.

Modifications of *65* and *64*

The *65* or *64* develop into outside plays when the tailback dips to the outside. A nice modification is a designed outside tailback play which starts with the *65* action, such as *67 Sweep* (Diagram 7-4). The tailback makes a *65* maneuver to the mesh

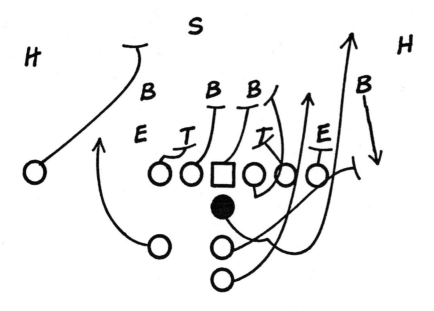

DIAGRAM 7-3: *Quick Right Split, 65 Blast Keep* **vs. 4-4**

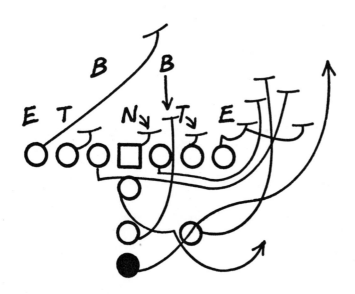

DIAGRAM 7-4: *I Right, 67 Sweep* **vs. 5-2 Strongside Slant**

point, then breaks outside in order to create a sideline stretch by the defense, turning upfield when he recognizes a seam. Either 67 or 66 *Blast* gives an opportunity to block a solid front while the fullback runs an arc 3 yards outside the tight end, driving the defender who breaks the arc to the outside.

The *63* and *62* Plays

The 63 and 62 plays are run with a direct pivot by the quarterback. On 63, the quarterback steps back with his right foot at 5 o'clock, making as deep a step as he can while he "third hands" the ball to his midsection. As the quarterback begins to follow with the second step, he extends the ball into the pocket of the tailback, carefully looking the ball in. He completes his second step, flattens his right foot to the *opposite* sideline on the third step, pretends he has the ball on his hip, moves to the outside as in a bootleg maneuver, checking the defensive containment and backside coverage. The tailback cheats slightly deeper in his alignment for 63. He steps with the right foot directly at the middle of the playside guard and makes his mesh with the quarterback on the second step. He accelerates for the hole, making any adjustments determined by his read of the defense. Usually the fullback will precede the tailback through the hole as in 63 *Blast* (Diagram 7-5). The tailback makes this an excellent cutback play by breaking to the other side if the defense overpursues.

It is possible to run the 63 *Double Blast* with a double team block on the nose guard, which is the old isolation play. We may run 63 *Straight Blast* by having all backside linemen block their numbers, enhancing the possibility of the cutback run. Another good possibility is the 63 *Double Straight Blast*, which puts the double team at the point of attack in combination with *Straight* blocking by the line. With three runners in the backfield, run 63 *Blast Wham*, 63 *Straight Blast Wham* (Diagram 7-6), or 63 *Double Straight Blast Wham*.

Efficiency of the 60 Series

The 60 Series is the basis of any *I* set. A tailback is set deep so that he can attack both sides equally well and can get the ball deep enough to read the blocking and make decisions based upon his reads. You can run excellent *Keeps* off 65 and 64 fakes,

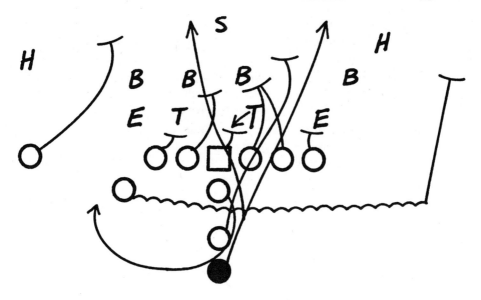

DIAGRAM 7-5: *I Star Split Zip, 63 Blast* vs. *Stunt 4-4*

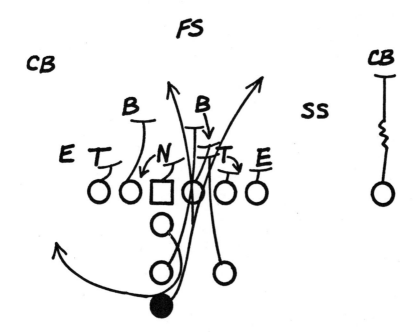

DIAGRAM 7-6: East, *63 Straight Blast Wham* vs. *5-2 Slant* Backside

as well as excellent sprint-out passes. The *63* and *62* fakes set up fine misdirection pass or run plays with the *Waggle* or *Bootleg* maneuvers.

The 60 Series can be efficient against almost any defensive front. Sound blocking fundamentals and a hard running tailback will force the defense to crowd you and overplay the tailback inside tackle. When that happens, use the keeps, the misdirection passes, and play passes to deceive the defense and make the big play. One or two of those big plays will make the defense play you honestly and once again give you the opportunity to undermine their defense. Overplaying the deliberate 60 Series can also set up the defense for quick hitting plays from other series.

chapter 8

Fullback's Delight: The Flexible 30 and 70 Series

T he 30 and 70 Series offer quick hitting thrusts by the full-back that are sequenced with counter plays by the other backs. These two series provide a good change of pace for the more deliberate 60 Series. They both rely on the fake of one play to precede or follow the designated play.

In the 30 Series (Diagram 8-1), the fullback hits the middle while the halfbacks flow to the odd side and the tailback counter steps, then flows odd.

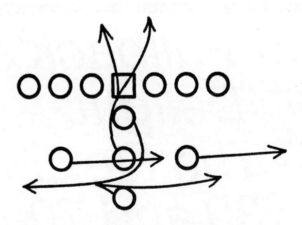

DIAGRAM 8-1: Flow Diagram for 30 Series—odd side

The 31 Plays

In 31 the fullback steps initially with the split-side foot at the split-side leg of the center. He takes the handoff from the quarterback and breaks according to the blocking. The quarterback puts his weight on his right foot and reverses quickly, insuring that he pivots far enough to permit the fullback to remain on his path; he must not force the fullback outside. The quarterback feathers the ball into the fullback's pocket, then steps back with the right foot, extends the left hand to the faking quick halfback (if there is one in the called set), then steps back with

76

the left foot and again the right foot. It is this third step back in which the quarterback flattens his foot to the opposite sideline, pretends he has the ball on his hip, and carries out a bootleg maneuver, checking the defensive containment and coverage to the backside. The *31 Straight* is illustrated in Diagram 8-2. The center blocks #0 by running through the numbers a bit softer than for a drive block. The fullback breaks opposite to the slip of the nose guard. A fine short yardage play is *31 Wedge*, which takes the blocking front to a point; if the fullback follows the wedge properly, he breaks to either side when he sees the opening. Make use of this play in normal yardage situations also; it can break for nice gains.

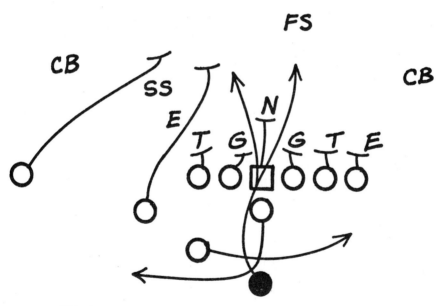

DIAGRAM 8-2: *A Pro-Board Split, 31 Straight vs. 6-1*

A favorite blocking scheme for *31* is *Trap* or *Pin* (Diagram 8-3). Through experience, the fullback learns to read the various trap breaks against different kinds of defenses. *Pin* is used more than *Trap* because today's linebacker reads the guard's down block, and the defensive tackle does not permit the offensive tackle to block down to the inside. The 30 plays are the reciprocals for *31*.

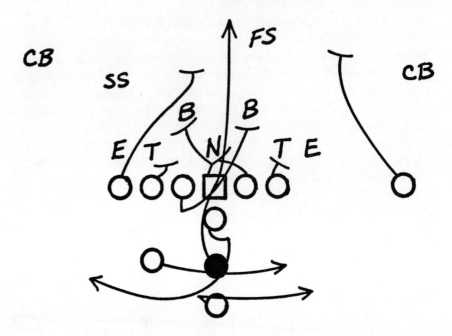

DIAGRAM 8-3: *Quick Right String, 31 Pin vs. 5-2*

The *35* and *34*

The *35* play is a good take-off from *31*. The fullback drives hard over the left leg of the center and executes a good fake. The quarterback moves his pivot as for *31*, but keeps the ball in his midsection. Because the quarterback and fullback pass so close to each other near the line of scrimmage, the quarterback does not make a fake to him. This reduces the chance of a fumble caused by the fullback's bumping the ball or the quarterback. The quarterback carries out his steps as in *31*, but extends the ball in his left hand to the quick halfback, then makes his boot-leg fake. The quick halfback open steps parallel to the line of scrimmage, receives the handoff from the quarterback, and adjusts his path to attack the off tackle hole. You can run *35 0* (Diagram 8-4) in which the split guard will trap #3 on odd and you will double team #2. The fullback fills for the pulling guard. The initial fake freezes the linebackers and there is good blocking at the point of attack. The *35 Base* or a variation

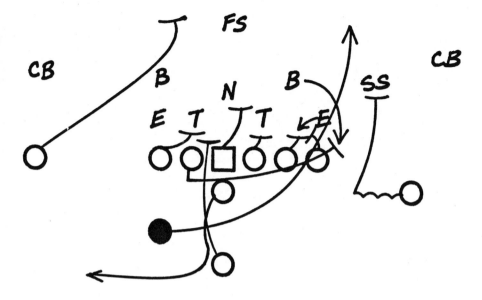

DIAGRAM 8-4: *A Gee Split Fly, 35 0 vs. 4-3 Stunt*

known as *35 Tear* can be run, in which the backside guard is pulled through the hole and blocks a solid front. The reciprocal play to the split side is *34*.

The same sequence can get you outside with *37 Tear, 37 Sweep,* or *39 Toss* (Diagram 8-5). These variations are incorporated if you need another way to get wide. The *38* plays are opposite.

Some years you will include the quarterback option play in your offense. Analyze your personnel, particularly your quarterback situation, before making a commitment to this play. It takes a great deal of practice to do the option well; unless you expect the play to pay big dividends, do not use it.

The *17 Veer*

The *17 Veer* is the Modular Offense version of the trap option (Diagram 8-6). It is a true three way read, and it takes a lot of work and a very skilled quarterback to produce worthwhile results. The quarterback makes his initial pivot as in *31*, hesitates for a half-second, then turns his shoulders to the odd side and

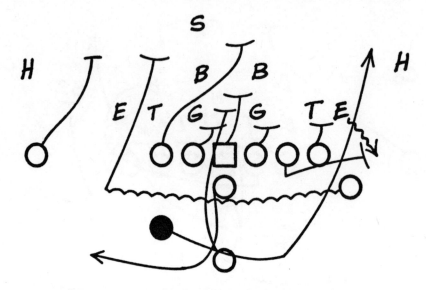

DIAGRAM 8-5: *A North Split Zip, 39 Toss* vs. wide *6*

proceeds to the sideline at a slight upfield angle. The quarterback reads the block of his backside guard on the defender outside the double team; if the offensive guard executes a trap block, the quarterback turns up inside the block and gains yardage. If the defender reads down and the guard logs him to the inside, the quarterback runs for the near shoulder of the next defender, and executes an option on him. If the option defender turns his outside shoulder to the offensive quarterback, the quarterback extends his right arm and turns his palm down to execute the pitch to the tailback. If the defender penetrates or moves outside quickly, the quarterback turns upfield and runs. The key coaching point is that the quarterback must force the feather end who slow plays the pitch to turn his shoulders in.

The Two Way Option

If the three way read is too complicated, or if you want the simpler two way option, consider *17 Kick*, in which there is no kick back but in which we have a double team with the end and tackle for an *Odd* call. This is on option on #3 (Diagram 8-7). We also run the option by calling *17 Base* with solid blocking against the front. Even the simplest option play requires a firm

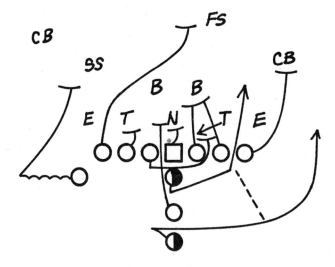

DEFENDER CLOSES –
OPTION NEXT MAN

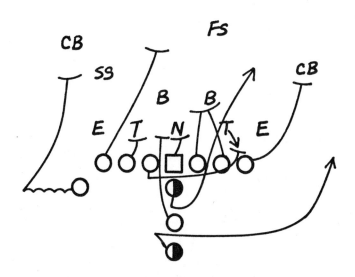

DEFENDER TRAPPED –
QB INSIDE

DIAGRAM 8-6: I Star Float, 17 Veer vs. 5-2

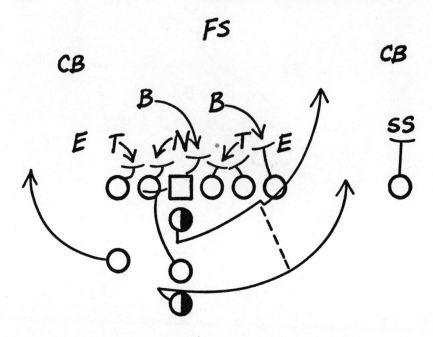

DIAGRAM 8-7: *Quick-East, 17 Kick* vs. *Stunt 5-2*

commitment on the part of the coaching staff to do the necessary work to perfect the play. The *16* plays are opposites for *17*.

The 70 Series

The 70 Series is a nice crossbuck *I* formation maneuver. It is
based on a quick opener by the fullback (Diagram 8-8) and the
counter by the tailback.

In *73* the fullback steps directly for the hips of the tight
guard, receives the handoff and breaks for the daylight. The
quarterback takes a short step, puts his right foot at 4 o'clock,
and extends the ball immediately to the fullback (he does not
have time to third hand the ball to his midsection). The trigger
man steps so that his left foot is even with his right foot, then
pivots on his left foot facing the opposite sideline and gives the
passing tailback a free hand fake. He then makes a seven step
drop. He starts and finishes the drop with his right foot. The
tailback steps at the hips of the guard with his right foot, gets
his shoulders forward, and hesitates slightly. The tailback

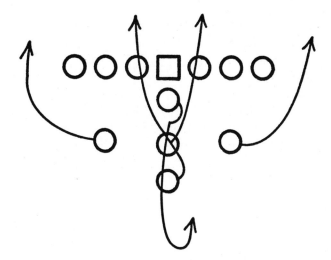

DIAGRAM 8-8: Flow Diagram for 70 Series—odd side

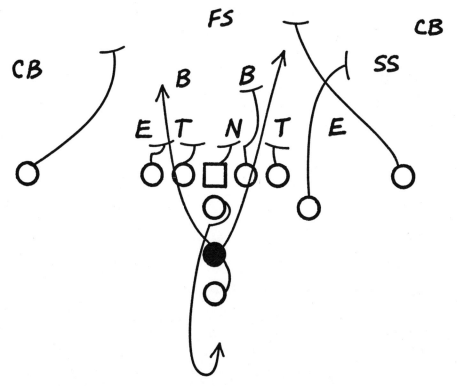

DIAGRAM 8-9: *I North Flex-Split, 73 Straight vs. 5-2 Overshift*

drives off the right foot directly for the hips of the backside guard, executing a good fake.

You can run *73 Straight* and *73 Base*. *73 Straight* gives you a little better opportunity to cut back (Diagram 8-9), but at the expense of missing the stunt to the backside. You can run a *73 Wham* if you have a halfback in the formation, but cheat his alignment up and to the inside to get him in front of your full-back (Diagram 8-10). A good variation is *73 Double Wham*. The 72 plays are the opposite of *73*.

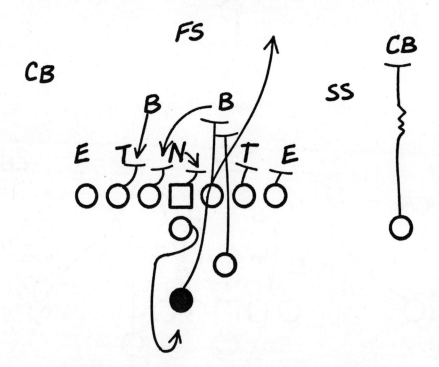

DIAGRAM 8-10: *B Gee, 73 Wham* vs. *5-2 Backside Stunt*

The *70 Counter*—a Misdirection Play

The *70 Counter* play is an excellent misdirection play (Diagram 8-11) set up by *73*. The quarterback makes his steps as for *73*, but does not fake to the fullback. The nearness of the two backs and their proximity to the line of scrimmage creates an effec-

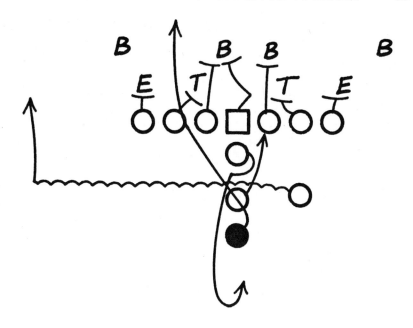

DIAGRAM 8-11: *I Right, Y Zig, 70 Counter vs. 4-4*

tive fake, making it unnecessary to take a chance and extend the ball or an open hand. The quarterback reverse pivots, steps with his right foot, and extends the ball to the tailback with his right hand. Upon execution of the handoff the quarterback makes his seven step drop. The *70 Straight* is a good call, driving the linemen into the defenders a little harder than *70 Counter* does. You can also run the *70* Trap. Another variation is *70 Hinge.* The *71* play is the opposite of *70*.

Another Misdirection Play

An additional aspect of the misdirection series is *74 Counter* (Diagram 8-12). The play is executed just like *70 Counter,* except that the tailback breaks to the outside for the off tackle hole. The *74 0* makes a good play, since you get a nice fill by the fullback. The series takes you outside when you run *76 Tear* by blocking a solid front, climbing the end on #3, and leading the backside guard. The *75* and *77* plays are the opposites for *74* and *76*.

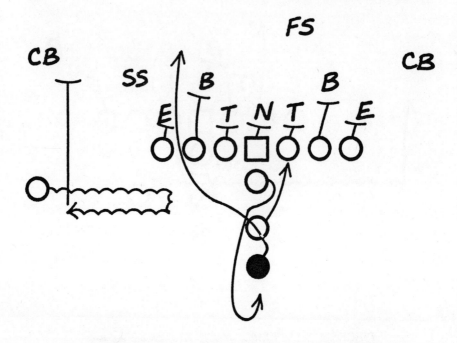

DIAGRAM 8-12: *I Pro Zap, 74 Counter vs. 5-2 Eagle*

The 30 and 70 Series combine deception with quick hitting plays and good blocking schemes. They are good fundamental ways to attack the defense.

When the defense gangs up on the quick hitting plays in these series, run the counter actions. They serve the dual purpose of making for effective gains and forcing the defense to play honestly. They add that irreplaceable ingredient, deception, to your attack.

9

Speed and More Speed: The Flexible 80, 40, and 20 Series

S peed is at a premium in football. The three series in this chapter feature quick opening plays into the line or fast plays to the outside. They provide opportunities for your running backs to use their speed to its greatest potential.

The 80 Series includes a quick burst to the middle by one of the halfbacks with fast flow to the outside by the other backs (Diagram 9-1). Every play in the series gets to the point of attack quickly.

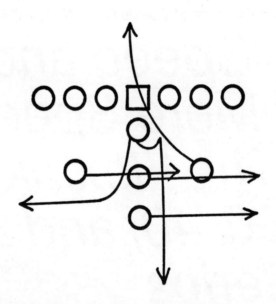

DIAGRAM 9-1: 80 Series—Flow Diagram—odd side

The Modern *Green Bay Sweep*

The *87* play may serve as a bread and butter play. The *87 Broom* (Diagram 9-2) is a modern version of the *Green Bay Sweep*. The *Broom* module has the end draw block #3. Sometimes this is altered to climb block #3, performing a counter block on him

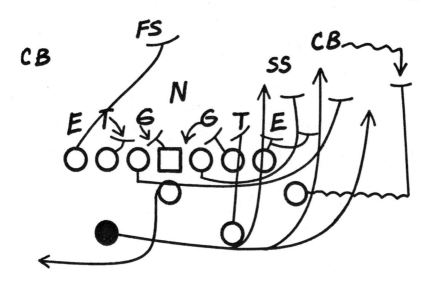

DIAGRAM 9-2: *D North Float, 87 Broom* vs. *Stunt 6-1*

and running with him to the sideline. The quick halfback open steps to the sideline and receives the handoff from the quarterback; he then bellies back slightly and slows up to read the blocking pattern. He stretches the defense, finds the alley, and accelerates upfield. The quarterback third hands the ball and reverse pivots, stepping deep to 6 o'clock with the left foot. He extends the ball to the quick halfback, steps with the right foot, flattens out with the left foot and fakes the bootleg.

The *87 Sweep* and *89 Toss*

When you have a fullback set you may choose to run *87 Sweep* (Diagram 9-3). A nice variation is *89 Toss;* you must beat the #2 man on the play. The *86* and *88* plays are the opposites for *87* and *89*.

The *85* is a designated off tackle play which starts like *87* but gets the running back upfield quickly. It is good to run *85 Kick* and *85 Power* (Diagrams 9-4 and 9-5), depending on the set you wish to use. The *85 Base* and *85 Wham* are good variations. The *84* is the opposite play for *85*.

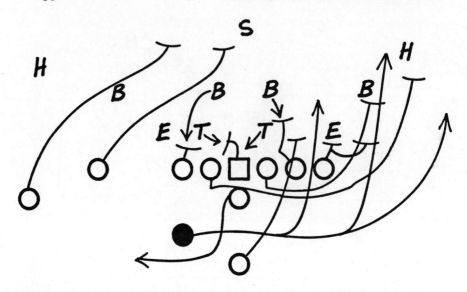

DIAGRAM 9-3: *A Pro-Pickle, 87 Sweep vs. Stunt 4-4*

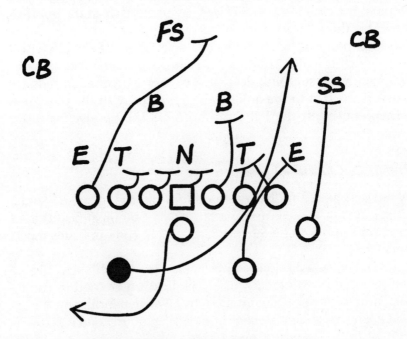

DIAGRAM 9-4: *D North, 85 Kick vs. 5-2*

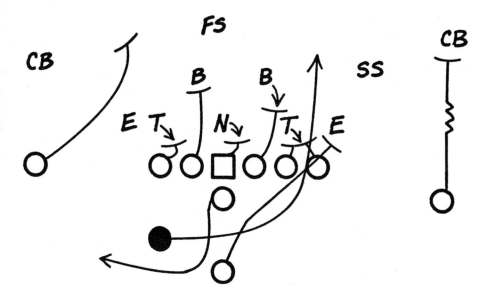

DIAGRAM 9-5: *A Gee-Split, 85 Power vs. 5-2 Slant*

The *80* and *81* Plays

The *80* play is a burst to the middle by the halfback. It is a fast counter to the flow of the other backs. You may run *80 Trap* (Diagram 9-6). The halfback steps directly toward the near leg of the center and runs that path until he gets the exchange from the quarterback. He breaks to the inside of the trapper. The quarterback reverse pivots, places the left foot a very short distance directly behind him at 6 o'clock, brings the other foot up even and extends the ball to the halfback. After he executes the handoff, the quarterback makes a seven step drop, starting and finishing with his right foot. He must make certain not to collide with other crossing backs on his drop. The *80 Pin, 80 Straight, 80 Hinge,* or *80 Counter* are variations sometimes used. The *81* plays are the opposite of *80.*

The *Quick Pitch* and Variations

The 40 Series is based on the *Quick Pitch* and a fast fullback off tackle play to complement the pitch (Diagram 9-7). Speed is used as a threat to get outside quickly or to loosen the outside of the defense, providing an opening at the off tackle hole.

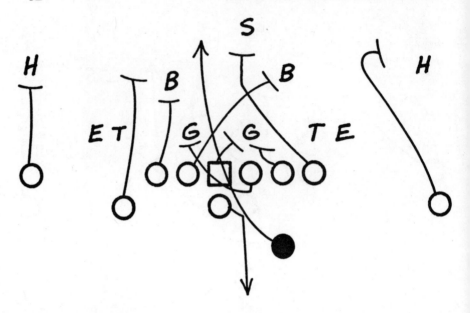

DIAGRAM 9-6: *L-D Gee Split, 80 Trap* vs. *Wide 6*

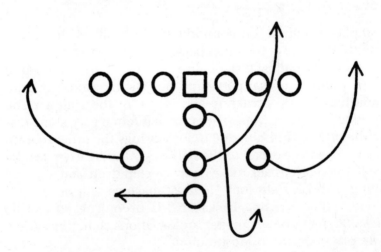

DIAGRAM 9-7: 40 Series—Flow Diagram—Odd Side

The *49 Toss* is run as a quick pitch play (Diagram 9-8). The halfback takes a step to the outside and back at a 45 degree angle. He should receive the ball on his second step, looking it into his midsection. After he tucks the ball away, the halfback looks for the blocking and makes his cut accordingly. The quarterback steps directly at the halfback with his right foot and extends the ball, making a soft two-hand toss at his target. The quarterback lands on his second step at the instant he releases the ball. He leaves his hands extended and places them in the pocket of the fullback. After the fullback clears, the quarterback makes a seven step drop, starting and finishing with the right foot. The fullback (if in position) runs directly for the inside leg of the end and makes a very large pocket for the ball. The pitch should pass just in front of his fake. The other backs swing to the opposite side. If you do not want to pull the tackle, run *49 Base*, blocking a solid front. The *48* is the opposite of *49*.

A sequential take-off from *49* is the *45 Base*. The quarterback and halfback fake the pitch and the fullback takes the handoff from the quarterback and adjusts his path according to the blocking in front of him. If you think the #3 man will be

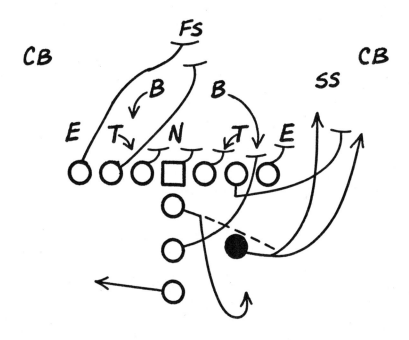

DIAGRAM 9-8: *I Right, 49 Toss vs. Stunt 5-2*

influenced by the halfback's outside move, you may run *45 Power* (Diagram 9-9). You can make a *Backer* call on the line and run *45 Base* without blocking the end. The opposite play for *45* is *44*.

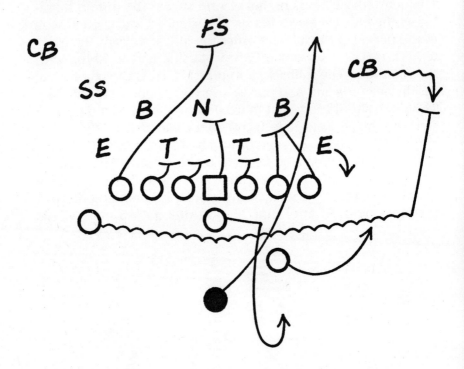

DIAGRAM 9-9: *B Star Zip, 45 Power* vs. *4-3*

The Conventional Dives and Their Offspring

The 20 Series is based on the straight dive play. One halfback executes the dive and the other backs flow to the side of the dive (Diagram 9-10).

The *23 Base* is the conventional dive (Diagram 9-11). The halfback runs straight ahead and makes his pocket. When he receives the ball, he adjusts his patch according to the blocking. The quarterback pushes off his left foot and takes a step upfield and to the right with the right foot. He makes a long crossover step with his left foot and extends the ball to the pocket of the halfback. When the halfback clears the quarterback, the quarterback continues on the line of scrimmage and fakes an option pitch to one of the flowing backs. Stress to the quarterback that

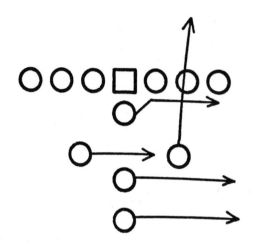

DIAGRAM 9-10: 20 Series—Flow Diagram—Odd Side

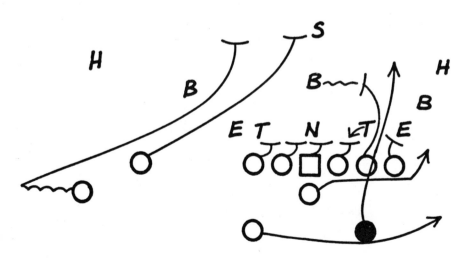

DIAGRAM 9-11: C Pro-Split Float, 23 Base vs. Slant 5-3

the ball is handed off on the line of scrimmage. This is an old play and one of the best in football. Its concept is simple, but it takes quality practice to develop it adequately. The *23 Straight* is also a good possibility. The *22* is the opposite of *23*.

Run *21 Straight* (Diagram 9-12) by directing the halfback for the inside leg of the guard. When he receives the handoff, he adjusts his path based on what he sees. The quarterback takes a 6 inch jab step parallel to the line with his right foot, comes up even with his left foot, and executes the handoff. After the handoff the quarterback proceeds down the line of scrimmage and fakes the option play. The *21* play frequently breaks to the backside, taking advantage of overpursuit by the defense. The *20* is the opposite of *21*.

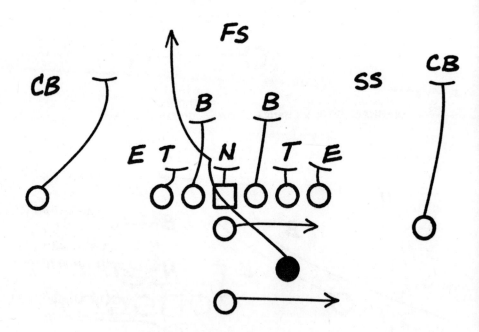

DIAGRAM 9-12: *B Gee-Split, 21 Straight vs. 5-2*

The outside dive or *25 Base* is sometimes incorporated (Diagram 9-13). The halfback runs at three-quarter speed for the outside leg of the tackle. He reduces his speed so that the quarterback can get the ball to him. The quarterback steps as in *23,*

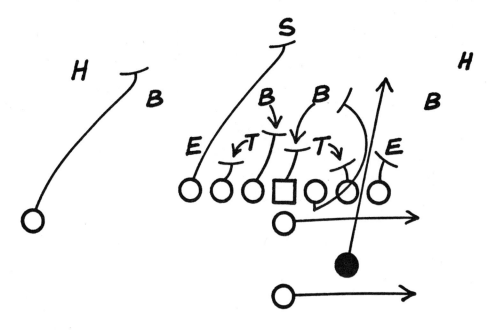

DIAGRAM 9-13: D-I Pro, 25 Base vs. 4-4

except that he is parallel to the line of scrimmage on his first step. He extends the ball on his second step and he will be moving on his third step when he executes the handoff. He fakes the option after the handoff. Emphasize deliberate moves by the halfback and quarterback on this play; it is still the fastest way to get off tackle. If you want to live dangerously, try *25 Power* (Diagram 9-14); if #3 is outside conscious, you will run past him. This gives you some of the aspects of the outside veer play.

The three series described in this chapter take advantage of speed at the point of attack. They get you there "firstest with the mostest."

Backs who develop quick starts are good dive backs and make the 20, 40, and 80 Series good plays. Quick hitting plays offer the advantage of getting into the secondary quickly; they are good choices against stunting defenses or defensive looks with the secondary up tight. Work on these speed series will pay dividends if you employ them against those attacking defenses.

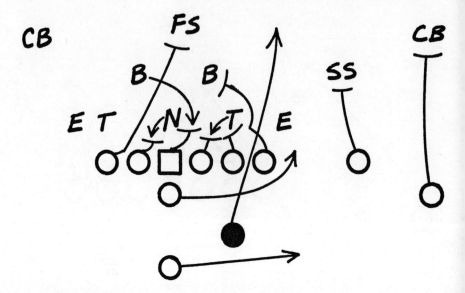

DIAGRAM 9-14: *B East-Gee, 25 Power* vs. *Stunt 5-2*

10

It Starts Here: Modules for Pass Protection

An outstanding passer, fine receivers, good coaching, and well conceived Xs and 0s will add up to an unsuccessful passing attack if you cannot protect your passer. Pass rush techniques are so good, and blitzing schemes are so varied, that pass protection is more difficult than ever. Dozens of different pass protection systems have been used. The present method of protection is based on the "pass it on zone" system which combines both aggressive and passive blocking techniques.

Techniques for Pass Blocking

The aggressive pass block is a drive block. You depend on the fake of the run to assist the blocker in his aggressive pass protection, or use that technique to get some room on the line of scrimmage, so you can throw the pass from that vicinity or get the quarterback to the outside. The blocker drives the defender and sustains contact as long as he can. He can not leave the line of scrimmage to block a linebacker.

The passive protection block is used on the back side of a play fake, or when you want the passer to set up in a fixed spot without a play fake. The blocker sets to block his defender with his hips low, in a good balanced position. He stays in front of the defender and aligns his hips so that they are perpendicular to a line drawn from the midline of his body to the passer. When the rusher is within striking distance, the blocker strikes out with the fists at the sternum area of the rusher. He strikes him with a two-hand punch with his elbows down. He resets and repeats this procedure, keeping his hips in proper alignment and maintaining his body in good hitting position. If the defender gets to a position on the hip of the blocker, the blocker executes a drive block by running through the far armpit of the defender. It is unlikely that a rushing lineman can run over the offensive lineman and get to the passer in time to disrupt the play. Consequently, the rule is stay in front and

100

strike out. Backs need forward momentum, since their targets have themselves gained momentum in their run into the backfield. The back takes two steps at the defender and strikes the sternum with his fists, recovers and executes the block properly. If he does not maintain proper position, he executes the drive block on the outside armpit. These are the fundamentals of pass blocking. The first step is for the coach to know them, but most important is teaching them to his players. No passing attack will be consistently successful without good protection.

Pull Protection

If you want to set up the passer directly behind a tackle at a depth of 8 yards, employ pull protection. All blockers perform passive techniques. The zone principle for this module will leave a seam between the center and the backside guard for which the lineman are not responsible. The center and the linemen on the front side of the pull have a rule which states "on, front side gap." This priority means that these blockers are assigned to a defender who penetrates through their position or to their play side gap. No one is responsible for his back side gap. Defenders who penetrate that gap are assigned to the next blocker. A vital coaching point is to insure that the blocker is conscious of who can penetrate his responsibility first. When the rusher leaves the blocker's priority area, the blocker passes him on to another blocker and prepares himself for a new rusher into his priority area. The back side guard and tackle are responsible for "on, back side gap." The back assigned to the front side blocks the first rusher outside his tackle's block, while the back assigned to the back side blocks anyone who penetrates the center guard gap.

Secondary assignments for blockers are used when no one challenges their assigned areas. Linemen will block any rusher who comes free to the outside (the center works to the front side).

Pull-Odd Protection

Diagrams 10-1, 10-2, 10-3, and 10-4 are examples of assignments for *Pull Odd* protection. *Pull Even* is the opposite.

In Diagram 10-1 the center is alert for the defender who is aligned on him; when he goes back side, the center picks up the linebacker coming to his play side gap. The front side guard is alert for the defender on his tackle, who can penetrate his play side gap very quickly. When the tackle goes to that alley, the guard blocks him. Remember, if the blocker does not maintain proper hip position, he executes a drive block by running through the outside armpit of the target. The front side tackle passes on the defensive tackle when he goes to his back side gap and picks up the stunting linebacker. The back side guard alerts for the tackle on his tackle; when he wipes to the outside and the linebacker also leaves his priority area, he picks up the twisting end coming through his back side gap. The back side tackle stays with the tackle, since no one rushes on or to the outside gap. The back responsible for the front side blocks the rushing end, while the other back blocks the rushing nose guard.

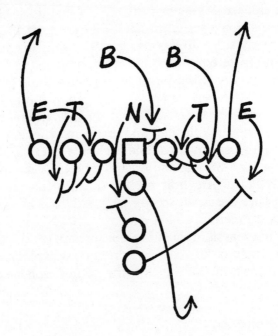

DIAGRAM 10-1: *Pull Odd* Protection vs. *Stunting* and *Twisting 5-2*

Diagram 10-2 illustrates pull protection against a *Wide Tackle 6* defense. Notice the center has no one rushing his zone, so he drops out to the front side and picks the first free man. The back responsible for the back side checks his gap, then picks up the first free man outside (in this case it is the end). Other blockers pick up rushers in their zones.

Diagram 10-3 demonstrates this zone system for pull protection against a *Split 4* with the entire front rushing. The center picks up the rushing linebacker to the play side, with the guard and tackle blocking the defenders rushing through their outside gaps. The play side back blocks the rushing end. The back assigned away from the pull blocks the linebacker coming through the guard center gap, while the guard, tackle, and end block to the back side. Notice that the back side end is blocking

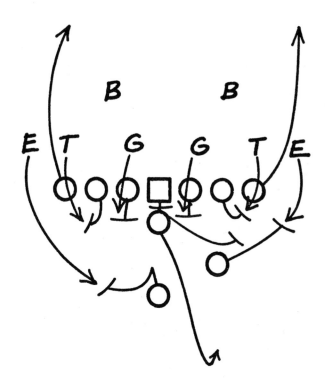

DIAGRAM 10-2: *Pull Odd* **Protection vs.** *Wide Tackle 6*

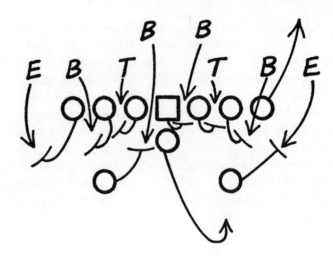

DIAGRAM 10-3: *Pull Odd* **Protection vs.** *Stunting Split 4*

in this situation. The pull module assigns seven blockers to pass block. If the opponent rushes more defenders than that, there are ways to handle the situation. One possibility is to make the quarterback aware of who the open rusher will be, and dump the ball off to a "hot" receiver if that rusher is harrying our passer. Another way to counteract the heavy rush is to add an extra blocker, either an end or a back. Incorporate the tight end into the protection by using the supplemental word "Hold," or we can use the split end in the protection by using "Stay."

Another view of pull protection is provided in Diagram 10-4. The front side tackle alerts for the end coming to his gap; when that does not occur, he picks up the blitzing linebacker. The back assigned to the back side picks up the linebacker who rushes the guard center gap.

Good scouting and thorough preparation will aid the coach in setting up pull protection. If you are concerned about an outstanding rusher or a particular rush alignment or stunt, you may rearrange the protection and "bump the seam." The blocking is set up so that you can leave any gap open. Diagram 10-5 depicts a module in which you leave the front side center guard gap open. The center adjusts his rule to "on, back side

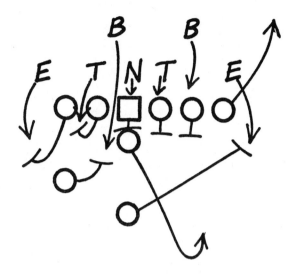

DIAGRAM 10-4: *Pull Odd* **Protection vs.** *Eagle, Reduced 5-2*

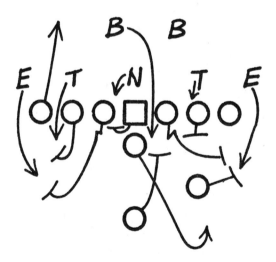

DIAGRAM 10-5: *Pull Odd* **Protection Module With Front Side Center Guard Gap Open**

gap"; the back ordinarily assigned to the back side checks the front side center guard gap, then checks to the back side. An enterprising coach tailors his zone protection to best fit a particular opponent. Recently football teams at all levels have combatted zone protection schemes by running a linebacker or a twisting lineman through a gap just behind an initial rusher. If you expect that, assign one of the backs as a lookout for such a maneuver while you "Hold" or "Stay" with one of the ends.

Drop Protection

The passer takes a seven step drop which puts him about 8 yards behind the center. The protection is as for *Pull Odd,* except that the blockers know that the passer sets up directly behind the center. Correct body position requires them to align so that their hips are perpendicular to a line drawn from the midline of the blocker's body to the quarterback. It is possible to adjust this protection just as the pull protection is adjusted (Diagram 10-6).

Sprint Protection

This module protects the passer who is on the move. He may make a hard sprint for the sideline, or he may move to the out-

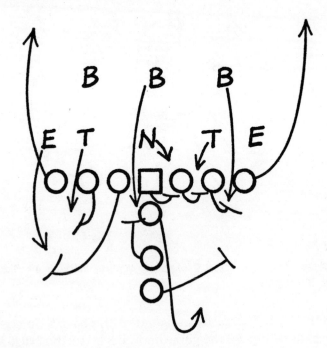

DIAGRAM 10-6: *Drop Protection vs. 5-3, Front Side Stunt*

side after a play fake. The front side blocks aggressively, the back side blocks passively. This is zone protection, and the seam is outside the back side tackle; the center adjusts his assignment so he drops to the back side if no one attacks his priorities. It is difficult for a heavy back side rush to catch the quarterback if he is moving quickly to the sideline.

The play side guard and tackle have a priority of "on, outside gap," but the blocking is aggressive. They drive block the outside armpit or hip of a defender who shows in the priority area. A blocker who is positioned in front of a bubble steps to the play side gap and aggressively blocks the priority area; if a linebacker takes a direct blitz, he turns back and blocks him. If no one shows in the priority area, these blockers check to the outside and block passively. The center has the same rule, except that he blocks passively to the backside if no one enters his priority area. The back side guard and tackle have the same rule as in *Pull* and *Drop*, except that they adjust their hip alignment to protect a passer who is rapidly moving to the opposite side. Again, a passive block becomes aggressive when the rusher is on the hip of a blocker. Diagrams 10-7 and 10-8 are examples of *Sprint Odd* protection. Usually one back is assigned as a blocker for sprint protection, and he blocks to the side of the play. The fullback runs a straight line directly for a point three yards outside the offensive end. Somewhere along that path, he will encounter a defender. He blocks the outside armpit aggressively. He accelerates his feet on contact and stays with the block as long as he can. Do not allow the fullback to attempt to position himself and make this a passive block.

Diagram 10-7 indicates the *Sprint* assignments against a *Stunting 5-2*. The center passes on the nose guard who goes to the back side gap; he picks up the linebacker coming to his front side gap. The guard steps hard to the play side gap and drives the outside hip of the slanting tackle. The play side tackle steps for the outside hip of the defender on him; when he disappears to the inside, the tackle drives the linebacker rushing over him. The back side guard must pick up the slanting nose guard. He will not be able to block him passively since he has inside position. It is necessary to drive block his far hip.

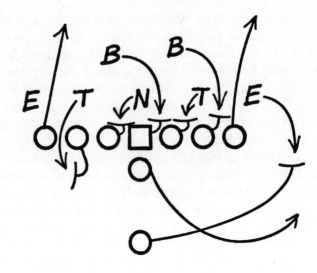

DIAGRAM 10-7: *Sprint Odd vs. Stunting 5-2*

In Diagram 10-8, the sprint protection is against a split 4 with the outside linebacker rushing from the back side. Notice the tackle picks up the linebacker and the center drops to block the rushing end. On the front side, the tackle has no one rushing his priorities, so he blocks to the outside.

Diagram 10-9 indicates the *Sprint Odd* versus a *Stunting Wide Tackle 6*. You depend on the fake to hold up the rush on a four man front side rush. If you are concerned that you may not be effective in blocking this four man rush side, you may have the fake back block after the fake. You can also assign an additional back to block the extra defender or call the playside end into the protection by adding "Hold" or "Stay" to the call. It is possible to block the backside with an additional man by using an extra back or calling the end into the protection to block passively. You can "bump the seam" on *Sprint* protection and make a multitude of adjustments to handle specific problems. In Diagram 10-10 the seam is moved to the front side guard tackle gap, and the tackle is assigned to his regular aggressive assignment. Both guards, the center, and the back side tackle are given passive assignments. An extra back picks up the front side guard tackle seam.

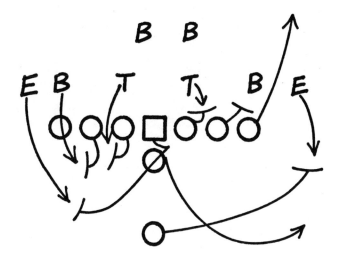

DIAGRAM 10-8: *Sprint Odd* vs. *Split 4*

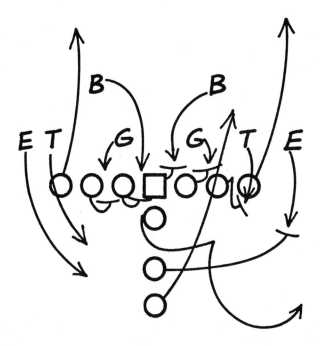

DIAGRAM 10-9: *Sprint Odd* Play Pass vs. *Stunting Wide Tackle 6*

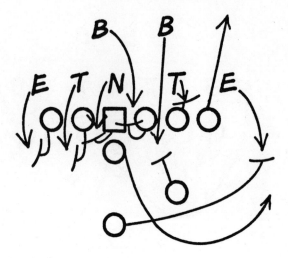

DIAGRAM 10-10: *Sprint Odd* Protection Module With Seam Bumped to Front Side Guard Tackle Gap

Hum Protection

This module is similar to *Sprint.* It protects the passer who is close to the line of scrimmage and throws to receivers executing quick cuts. There may or may not be a play fake. The front side blocks as in the *Sprint,* while the back side has *Sprint* assignments using aggressive techniques. You want to knock the defenders off the line of scrimmage and keep their hands down. An example of *Hum Protection* is shown in Diagram 10-11.

Boot Protection

This module is designed for quarterback movement away from a play fake. You want to throw on the run, although the quarterback may be forced to set up. For *Boot,* the guard on the fake side pulls to the opposite side at a 45 degree angle; if he spots a penetrator he executes a drive block through the outside armpit. If there is no penetration the guard turns upfield behind his end's original position. He blocks the first defender to show. If he hears the quarterback yell "go" the guard leads the play, making it a run. On both sides the tackle and end block aggres-

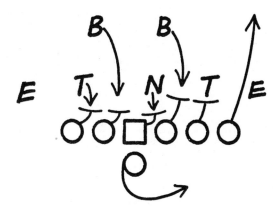

DIAGRAM 10-11: *Hum Odd Protection* vs. *Double Gap Stack*

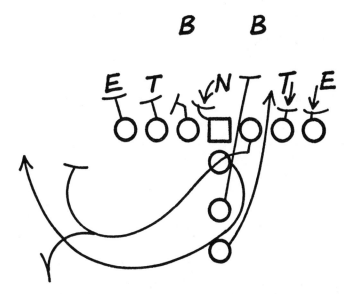

DIAGRAM 10-12: *Boot Even Protection* vs. *5-2*

sively. The priority is on, outside gap. The center makes an aggressive block on, boot side gap; if no one rushes his priorities, he blocks passively to the fake side. You may fill for the pulling guard with a faking back. Diagram 10-12 is an example of *Boot Protection:* The boot side guard has the sprint rule.

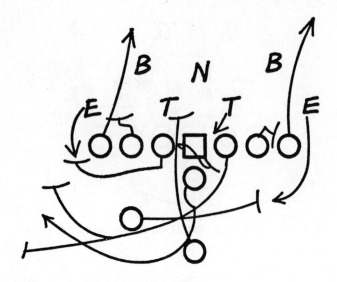

DIAGRAM 10-13: *Waggle Even Protection vs. College 4-3*

Waggle Protection

The *Waggle* module is similar to *Boot Protection.* Both guards pull and both ends are in the pass pattern. The *Waggle* side guard pulls flat and attacks the defender outside the tackle's block as quickly as possible. You want to block this defender on the line of scrimmage. The blocker runs through the defender's outside armpit. The fake side guard pulls, as in *Boot Protection,* and carries out the same assignment. You usually fill for the *Waggle* side guard with a back. An example of the *Waggle* module is illustrated in Diagram 10-13.

The *Waggle* and *Boot Protection* systems are not technically as sound as *Sprint, Hum, Pull,* or *Drop,* but a good fake, particularly in a run situation, will take a lot of heat off the quarterback.

chapter 11

Modular Pass Routes

P

ass routes are combined into specific patterns in order to get receivers open. The pass play is structured so that the passer gets to the proper launch point with good protection, and a running fake and/or a receiver pattern module takes advantage of the coverage.

Individual pass cuts are divided into three categories: (1) wide receiver routes, (2) normally spaced end routes, and (3) backfield routes.

Wide Receiver Routes

Wide receivers use a three point stance or an upright stance with the inside foot slightly back. For the out route, the receiver breaks from the line of scrimmage under control for a few steps, then accelerates upfield. When he gets to a depth of about 9 yards, he sinks his hips and comes under control again. At 12 yards, the receiver plants the inside foot and breaks to the outside at a right angle. He accelerates out of the break and gets his head around quickly, looking for the ball. A sharp break is critical for this route. If the receiver rounds the cut, the defender can react and get underneath the break more easily.

The corner route is a deeper version of the out. The receiver comes under control at about 13 yards and makes his break to the outside at 17 yards. The nifty athletes make the break at an angle greater than 90 degrees, coming back to the ball at a depth of 16 yards.

The *Curl* and the *Strike*

The *Curl* is a cut to the inside at a depth of 12 yards. The receiver accelerates to a depth of about 9 yards, sinks his hips, then plants the outside foot and breaks to the inside. He can hit this break at a greater speed than the out or the corner, since this cut is rounded. The receiver adjusts his curl by getting his head around and checking the underneath coverage man. If the defender is working out toward the receiver, the wide out finishes his curl so he gets inside the defender. If the under-neath defender is not working wide enough to get under the curl, the receiver brings his curl up short. In finishing the curl, the receiver comes back to the ball. A lot of good repetitions of quarterback-receiver reading this route will help to make it successful.

The *Strike* is a deeper version of the *Curl*. It is run in the same manner, except the break to the inside is at a depth of 17 yards. Diagram 11-1 shows *Out*, *Corner*, *Curl*, and *Strike* routes.

Quick Out and Slant In

The *Quick Out* is a break to the outside on the fourth step. The receiver steps off with the inside foot first and turns out on the fourth step. He goes into this break as fast as he can. Because this is such a short break he can hit it at full speed and turn on the outside foot to make his 90 degree cut. The receiver gets his head around quickly to look for the ball.

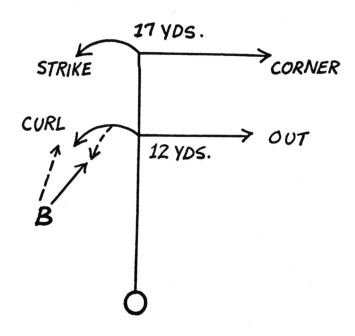

DIAGRAM 11-1: *Out, Corner, Curl,* **and** *Strike* **Routes**

The *Slant In* is a four step break which the receiver hits quickly on the outside foot. After the break to the inside he comes under control and angles his way into the open. The reference angle is 45 degrees, but he adjusts that angle according to the coverage.

The *Cross*

The *Cross* is a break to the inside at an angle of about 30 degrees. The receiver comes under control after the break and adjusts his angle according to the coverage. The break point for the route is at 10 yards. The receiver comes under control at about 7 yards and plants his outside foot for the break.

The *Q*

The *Q* is a complement for the *Quick Out*. The receiver breaks into a *Quick Out;* he stops himself on the second step of the outside leg, then shuffles slowly back to the inside with his shoulders square to the line of scrimmage, adjusting his angle according to the coverage. *Cross, Slant In, Quick Out*, and *Q* are illustrated in Diagram 11-2.

The *Post, Flag*, and *Deep*

The *Post* is a break to the inside at a depth of 14 yards. The receiver sinks his hips at about 11 yards, plants his outside foot and accelerates to the inside, aiming to split the goal posts. He wants to achieve an inside position so that he can catch the ball at about 30 to 40 yards deep. If the receiver recognizes that a defender is rolling from the back side or going straight back to cover the deep middle, he breaks off the post to a curl. This curl is at a depth of 20-25 yards.

The *Flag* is a break to the outside at a depth of 14 yards. The receiver drops his hips and plants the inside foot, then accelerates at an angle to the outside. He makes the cut so the outside leg is directed at the corner goal line flag. If he runs the route properly it will not take him out of bounds.

Deep is run by sinking the hips slightly at a depth of 14 yards, then taking a slight "wrinkle" to the outside, and accelerating upfield. The receiver makes certain that he does not bend his *Deep* to the inside. We want him to proceed di-

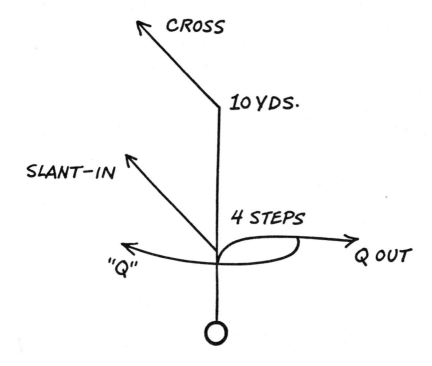

DIAGRAM 11-2: *Cross, Slant In, Quick Out,* **and** *Q* **Routes**

rectly upfield. If he is wrong, we want him wrong to the outside away from deep coverage help from the inside. Diagram **11-3** illustrates the *Post, Flag,* and *Deep* routes.

The *Under*

There is a route that is known as *Under* that does not belong to the other families of breaks. The wide receiver who runs this route is generally in a wing or board position. The receiver breaks from the line at an angle to the outside (about 30 degrees). When he gets to a depth of 8 yards, he plants the outside foot and works inside parallel to the line of scrimmage. He runs this inside leg under control, adjusting his angle and speed according to the coverage. *Under* is shown in Diagram **11-4.**

Routes for Normally Aligned Ends

Because of their spacing, ends positioned in normal alignments have some routes different from the wide receivers. These re-

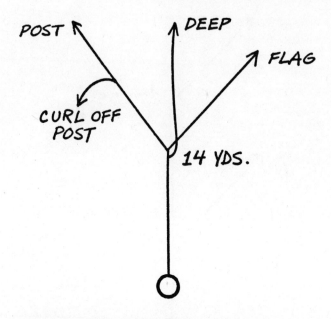

DIAGRAM 11-3: *Post, Flag,* and *Deep* **Routes**

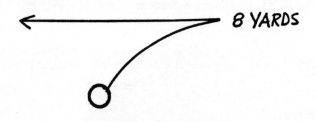

DIAGRAM 11-4: *Under*

ceivers must release in traffic and run breaks that are comple-
mentary to those of the wide receivers and backs.

Ends are coached to run *Flat, Out,* and *Cross* routes the
same as the wide receivers. Because of the congestion when
leaving the line of scrimmage, the ends must learn how to adjust in order to effect these routes.

In the *Squirrel* route, the departure from the line is at a 45
degree angle to the outside. The end establishes eye contact
with the quarterback on the fourth step of the route. When he

gets a depth of 8 yards he flattens out and runs parallel to the line of scrimmage at top speed. He stops and waits for the ball 1 yard from the sideline.

For *Bend*, the end releases to the outside at a 45 degree angle. He flattens out at 12 yards and proceeds at top speed.

On *Release*, the end steps to his outside directly toward the sideline for three steps, plants the outside foot, then turns upfield. As soon as he turns upfield he looks to the inside for the quarterback. The end tilts slightly to the outside to get away from the inside linebacker. He runs under control until he gets to a depth of 12 yards, at which point he turns to the outside and stops. If the ball is not delivered soon after the receiver stops, he may float to an open area.

For *Alley*, the end comes off the line slightly to his inside. He looks for the ball as quickly as he can and runs under control upfield at a slight angle to the inside. The receiver adjusts his angle according to the coverage.

The *Drag* route requires the end to come off the line to his inside. He looks to the quarterback immediately and runs under control to a spot 5 yards upfield from where the ball was snapped. At that depth he runs parallel to the line and under control. He stops 1 yard from the sideline.

Lift is the same as *Drag* except that the end stops at a depth of 5 yards. If he does not receive the ball right away, he floats for an open area. *Release, Squirrel, Bend, Drag, Lift* and *Alley* are shown in Diagram 11-5.

Backfield Routes

Include backs in the passing attack. This gives you more flexibility and an alternate receiver to dump to if our other receivers are covered or if the rush is too great. It also provides an additional burden for the opposition's defensive preparation. These routes may be run from fullback, either halfback, or tailback.

In *Flat*, the back runs to the end's position and works to a depth of 5 yards. At that point he flattens out and runs parallel to the line of scrimmage. You want him to run this route at top speed. He stops 1 yard from the sideline.

For *Circle*, the back runs to the end's position and turns upfield. As soon as he clears the line he looks to the inside for

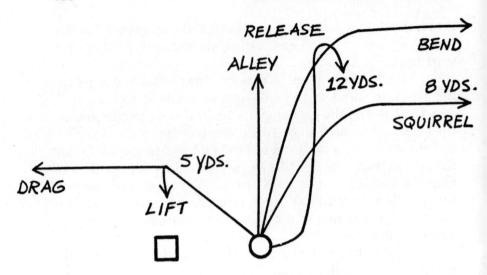

DIAGRAM 11-5: *Release, Squirrel, Bend, Drag, Lift,* and *Alley* **Routes**

the ball. He stops at a depth of 5 yards. If he does not receive the ball immediately, he floats to a free area.

Swing is the same as *Circle* except that the back turns upfield 5 yards outside the end. Instruct him to look over the inside shoulder as he progresses to the outside in the initial part of the route.

Spike is the same as *Swing* except that the back turns upfield when he is 10 yards outside the end.

Shoot takes the back to the end's position, where he flattens out and runs to the sideline, looking for the ball all the way. He runs under control and stops one yard from the boundary.

Up is a route in which the back runs the circle path at full speed and does not look for the ball until he gets fifteen yards past the line of scrimmage. This is a long pass route.

Flat, Circle, Swing, Spike, Shoot, and *Up* are depicted in Diagram 11-6. You can modify *Circle, Swing,* and *Spike* by adding "Go" to the route call. This will tell the back to keep working upfield, running under control and looking for the ball all the way. If you wish to design the protection and patterns so that the backs will remain and block for a heavy rush, prefix the route call with "Check." This assigns the back to check and block his first priority protection assignment, then his second priority protection assignment, then execute his pass route.

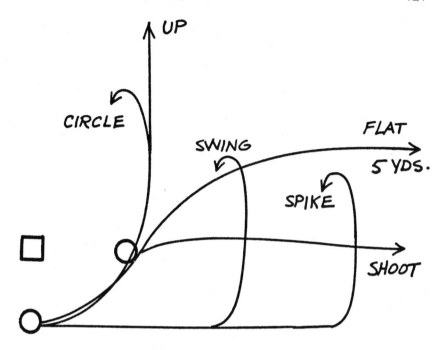

DIAGRAM 11-6: *Flat, Circle, Swing, Spike, Shoot,* and *Up* **Routes**

Groundwork Pass Routes

Take great care in teaching pass routes. They are the ground-work. Next in the progression is combining pass routes to give pattern modules which, added to protection modules and backfield actions, complete the passing game.

It is important to mention that wide receiver routes are carried out a bit more deliberately on a play fake pass than on a pass play without a run fake. The wide receiver approaches the defender and makes a quick feint as if to stalk the defender, then breaks into his route. The objective is to deceive the covering defender and cause him to think "run."

chapter 12

Pass Play Modules

The following explains in detail how to execute some basic patterns. The creative coach can modify these patterns to suit his personnel, to satisfy his personal preferences, and to probe the opponent's defensive coverage. There are endless possibilities for the Modular Offense passing game.

Calling Pattern Modules

The pattern module applies to the side of the call, designated as odd or even. Diagram 12-1 is a summary of some possible pass pattern modules.

The *Boot*

The *Boot* pattern instructs the Z back on the side of the call to run a *Flag/Out* route. He reads the coverage and runs an *Out* if the defender covering him has a good cushion. If he breaks the cushion, the receiver runs a *Flag* route. If the Z back aligns away from the call, he runs a *Cross* to the call side. The quarterback checks the coverage. *Boot Even* is shown in Diagram 12-2.

The *Waggle*

Waggle directs the Z back or the wide receiver (possibly a split end) on the call side to run the *Flag/Out*. If there are two receivers on the *Waggle* side, the outside receiver runs deep and the inside receiver runs an *Out*. The end away from the *Waggle* runs a *Drag* and the Z back away from the call runs a *Post*. The quarterback reads the coverage as in *Boot*; he has a nice secondary target in the dragging end. *Waggle Even* is illustrated in Diagram 12-3.

The *Strike and Squirrel*

The *Strike and Squirrel* combination takes advantage of the underneath coverage on the outside. The Z back runs a *Strike* and

124

Pattern	Call Side		Back Side	
	Z Back	End	Z Back*	End
Boot	Flag/Out	Block	Cross	Block
Waggle	Deep†	Flag/Out Out if on Z Back side	Post	Drag
Strike and Squirrel	Strike	Squirrel	Post	Lift
Corner and Release	Corner	Release	Post	Lift
Curl and Flag	Curl	Flag	Post	Lift
Deep and Out	Deep	Out	Post	Lift
Flag and Bend	Flag	Bend	Post	Lift
Back Side Curl	Post	Drag	Curl	Flag
Slant In	Slant In	Alley	Slant In	Alley
Flood	Deep	Bend	Post	Lift‡
Flag/Out	None	Flag/Out	Post	Cross
Under	Under	Out	None	Out
Q and Bend	Q	Bend	Post	Lift

*Also for wide spaced end that side
†Deep only for Z back on Waggle side
‡Nearest back runs flat

DIAGRAM 12-1: Summary of Pass Pattern Modules

the end runs a *Squirrel*. The quarterback reads the second deep defender (4 yards or deeper) from the outside in. If that defender backs up for the *Strike*, the quarterback delivers the ball to the *Squirrel* receiver. If the defender is moving to the outside, the pass is thrown to the *Strike* receiver. The quarterback and the wide receiver team up to read the linebacker coming out to cover the *Strike*. If he gets enough width, the receiver finishes up the *Strike* to the inside of the linebacker. If the linebacker does not get much width, the receiver pulls up short

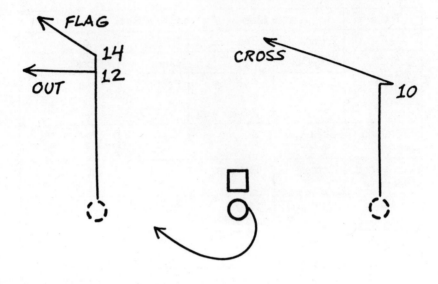

DIAGRAM 12-2: *Boot Even*

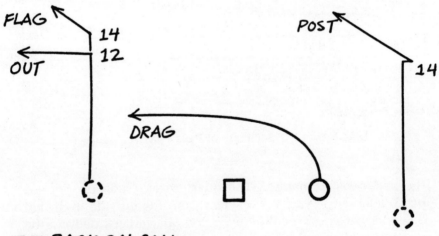

IF Z BACK ON CALL
SIDE, COMBINATION
IS DEEP AND OUT

DIAGRAM 12-3: *Waggle Even*

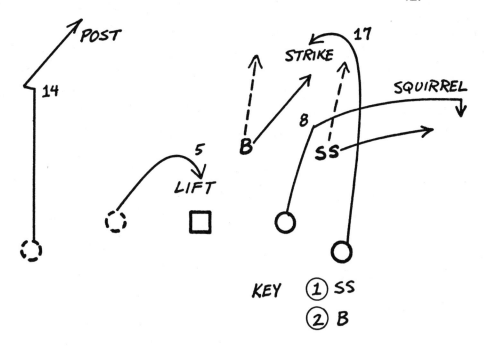

DIAGRAM 12-4: *Strike and Squirrel Odd*

for the *Strike*. If the quarterback is hung up, he delivers the ball late to the *Squirrel* man on the sideline or to the back side receiver. The normally spaced end on the back side runs a *Lift* while the wide receiver on the back side runs a *Post*. Diagram 12-4 is the *Strike and Squirrel*.

The *Corner and Release*

Corner and Release fits well with *Strike and Squirrel*. The Z back runs a corner route, with the end making his release. The quarterback keys the outside defender. If the defender is pushed off deep, the passer completes the *Corner*. If the defender does not have a cushion, the quarterback finds the end on the release. He can go back side if necessary. Diagram 12-5 shows the *Corner and Release*.

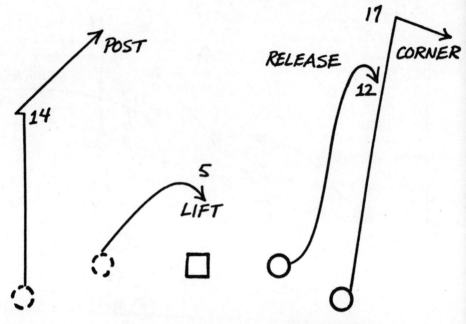

DIAGRAM 12-5: *Corner and Release Odd*

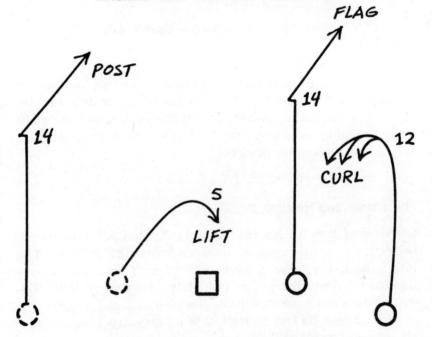

DIAGRAM 12-6: *Curl and Flag Odd*

The *Curl and Flag*

Curl and Flag is a pattern in which we read the outside deep defender. If the outside defender has a small cushion, we hit the end on the *Flag*, away from the deep middle coverage. If the defender has a good cushion, we hit the *Curl*. The receiver and quarterback read the *Curl* according to the underneath coverage. Diagram 12-6 illustrates the *Curl and Flag*.

The *Back Side Curl*

Back Side Curl is a pattern in which the wide receiver on the back side runs the *Curl* and the opposite end runs a *Drag*. A normally spaced back side end or an inside twin on that side runs a *Flag*. The wide receiver on the opposite side runs a *Post*. You usually run this pattern away from a backfield action or as a throwback by the quarterback. Diagram 12-7 shows the *Back Side Curl*.

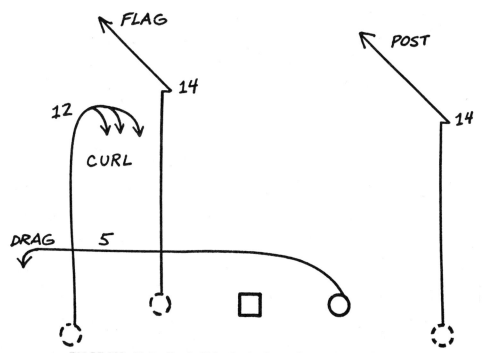

DIAGRAM 12-7: *Back Side Curl*—Away From Odd Call

The *Slant In*

Slant in assigns the outside wide receivers to run a *Slant in* and normally spaced ends to run an *Alley*. If there is a *Twins* alignment, the inside twin runs a *Release*. This play is in Diagram 12-8.

The *Flood*

Flood is designed to get receivers into open areas quickly. The wide receiver on the side of the call runs deep; the end executes a *Bend* and the closest running back makes a flat route. The back side end runs a *Lift* if normally spaced, and the wide receiver runs a *Post*. The pattern is shown in Diagram 12-9.

The *Flag/Out*

Flag/Out is similar to the *Waggle* call, but is always executed to a single receiver side. The receiver on the call side executes a *Flag/Out*. The end away from the call runs a *Cross*, and the Z back runs a *Post*. The quarterback reads the second deep defender from outside in on the call side. If he goes to the middle, the quarterback throws to the receiver running the *Flag/Out*. If the defender goes to the call side, the passer hits the Z back on the *Post* or the *Curl* off the *Post*. The Z back bases his decision on whether or not to break the *Post* deep on the reactions of the man responsible for deep middle coverage. He simply looks to the deep middle and continues on to the *Post* if no one is there. If he recognizes deep middle coverage, he breaks off the *Post* into a *Curl* maneuver. This play is diagrammed in 12-10.

ALLEY   ALLEY

SLANT IN   SLANT IN

4 STEPS   4 STEPS

DIAGRAM 12-8: *Slant In*

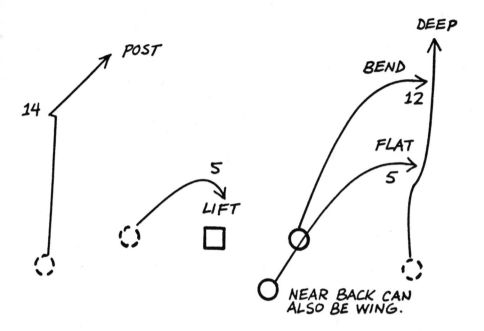

DIAGRAM 12-9: *Flood Odd*

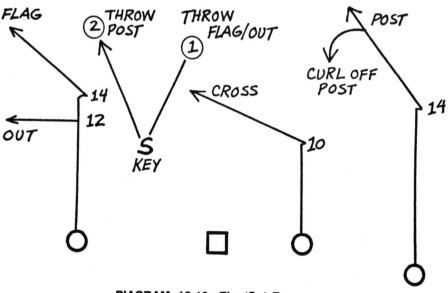

DIAGRAM 12-10: *Flag/Out Even*

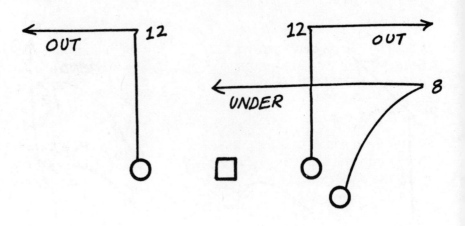

DIAGRAM 12-11: *Under*

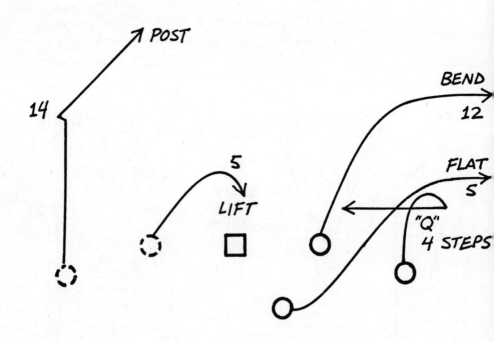

DIAGRAM 12-12: *Q and Bend Odd*

The *Under*

For *Under*, the Z back executes an *Under* and both ends run an
Out. The idea is to split the inside underneath coverage with a
nice soft pass, indicated in Diagram 12-11.

The *Q and Bend*

Q and Bend is a complement for *Flood*. The wide receiver runs
the *Q* and the end runs a *Bend*. The closest back runs a *Flat*,
with the back side end running a *Lift*. If a wide receiver is back
side, he runs a *Post*. This is shown in Diagram 12-12.

The *Delay*

For the *Delay* all receivers except the designated position run
deep routes. The tight end, halfback, fullback, or tailback can
run the *Delay*. Whoever is designated blocks according to his
module for three counts, then maneuvers into an open area in
the middle at a depth of 5 yards. For delay, the receiver always
comes from the tight side, as in Diagram 12-13.

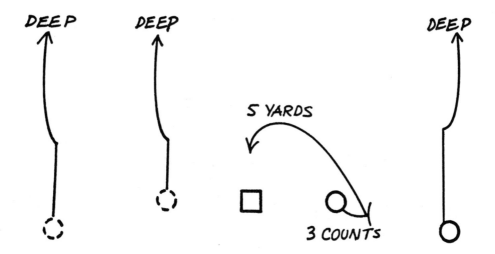

DIAGRAM 12-13: Tight End Delay

The *Late*

The *Late* is the reciprocal of *Delay*, clearing the receiver through the split side.

Protection and pattern modules are combined with pass actions to define some interesting pass plays. An enterprising coach can put together endless combinations for effective passing. Make careful selections and design a basic system that will suit your purposes.

Sprint Modules

Sprint Odd Flood is a short sprint out by the quarterback. He levels out on the third step and turns upfield. If he gets no rush pressure, he runs the ball. He signals the running by yelling "Go," making his receivers into blockers. If the quarterback gets an outside rush, he passes to the back or the tight end, depending on the coverage. The play is shown in Diagram 12-14.

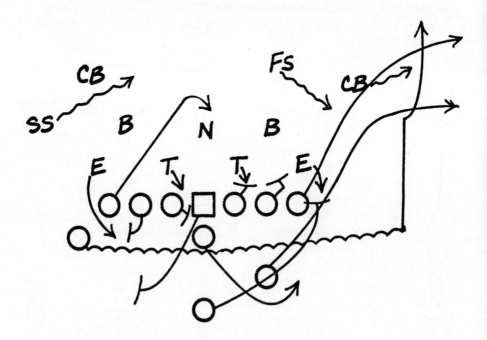

DIAGRAM 12-14: *B Star Zip, Sprint Odd Flood vs. 4-3*

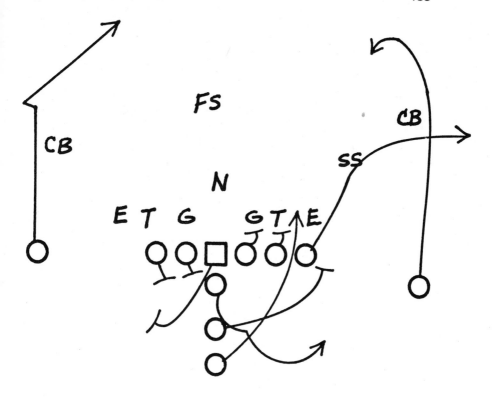

DIAGRAM 12-15: *I Gee Split, 65 Sprint, Strike and Squirrel vs. 6-1*

The *65 Sprint, Strike, and Squirrel* is shown in Diagram 12-15. You block sprint protection and the quarterback makes an open hand fake to the tailback for the *65* action, levels out on the fifth step, and turns upfield. The pattern is *Strike and Squirrel*. There are many other patterns possible off *65* or *64 Sprint*. You may include *Corner and Release, Deep and Out, Out and Flag, Curl and Flag, Flag and Bend,* among others.

Pull Modules

For a *Pull,* the passer takes seven steps to set up behind the call side tackle. The passer leans back to the line of scrimmage and plants hard with the sixth step, bringing him up tall and steady on step seven. *Pull Odd* sets up the right hander ready to pass. For *Pull Even*, the right hander must set up and reverse himself. The good quarterback looks into the coverage on his way back to set up.

Several patterns are run from the *Pull*, including all those mentioned in *65* or *64 Sprint*. The *Pull* is good to set up and throw to the back side. Two *Pull* pass plays are illustrated in Diagrams 12-16 and 12-17. A *63* tailback action is run in Diagram 12-17. This is not a true running fake, since the protection module is passive and the fullback is pass blocking, but the movement by the tailback may freeze the linebackers long enough to open the back side *Curl* lane.

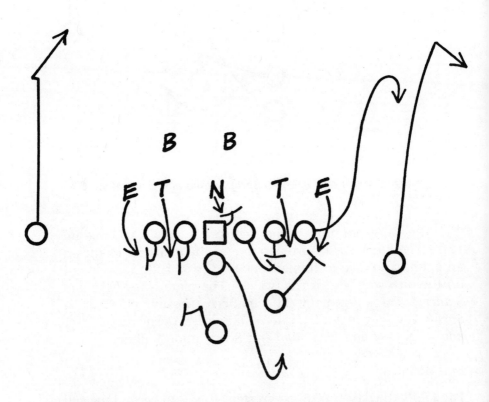

DIAGRAM 12-16: *B Gee Split, Pull* Odd, *Corner and Release* vs. *Double Gap Stack*

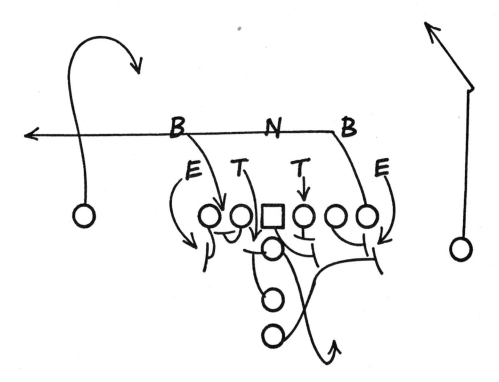

DIAGRAM 12-17: *I Gee Split,* **63 Pull—Back Side Curl vs.** *Stunting 4-3*

Drop Modules

For the *Drop*, the quarterback turns to the side of his dominant arm and drops back seven steps, setting up just behind the center, using the same technique as for the *Pull*. Designate the pattern odd or even or you can drop with a particular backfield action, such as *70* or *35*. Examples of *Drop* plays are shown in Diagrams 12-18 and 12-19. You can make the *Drop* or *Pull* modules more sophisticated by putting the backs into the pattern, with *Delay, Late, Check,* or calling a back into the pattern by using *Hold* or *Stay* for an end. It is also possible to immediately release backs on these patterns and have the quarterback read the blitzing linebackers as in Diagram 12-20. This is a sophisticated modification, and it takes a great deal of quality practice time to make it effective.

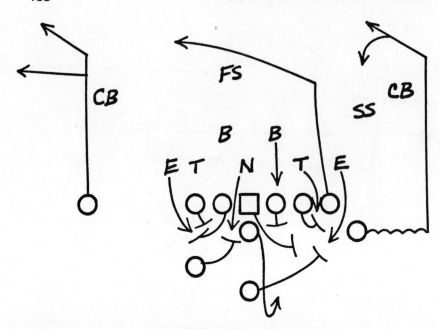

DIAGRAM 12-18: *A North Split Float, Drop, Flag/Out Even vs. Stunting 5-2*

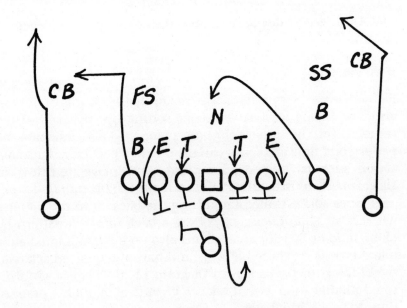

DIAGRAM 12-19: *Pro Flex, Y Gee, Drop, Deep and Out Even vs. Pro 4-3*

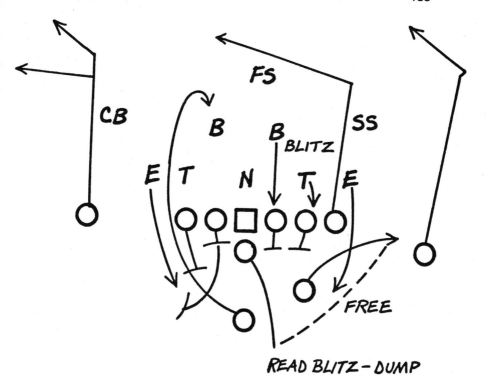

READ BLITZ – DUMP

DIAGRAM 12-20: *B Gee-Split, Drop, Flat-Out Even, Circle and Shoot* **vs.** *5-2 Blitz*

Boot Modules

Diagram 12-21 is an example of a *Boot* play. The quarterback makes the play fake, levels out to the opposite side on the third step (he can level out on the fifth step if we want him to). If there is no outside pressure, the passer yells "Go" and it is a run. It is best to throw the ball on the run. If the contain pressure is immediate, the passer sets up and throws. You can *Boot* off a number of different play actions, such as *70, 85, 63,* or their reciprocals.

Waggle Modules

This is the same idea as *Boot,* except both ends are in the pattern and the blocking is a bit different. You can run this from many actions. Diagram 12-22 is one example.

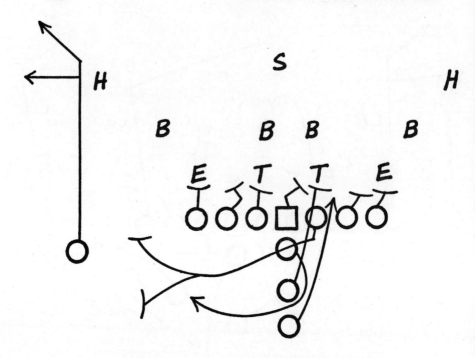

DIAGRAM 12-21: *I Pro 63 Boot Even* vs. *Split 4*

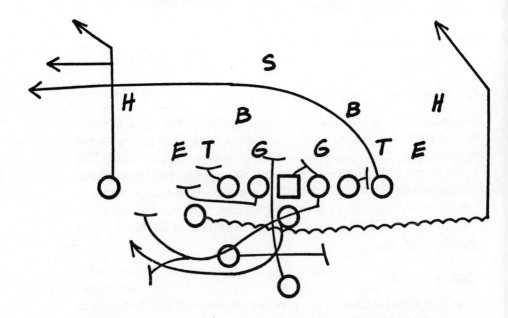

DIAGRAM 12-22: *A Star Split-Zip, 35 Waggle Even* vs. *Wide Tackle 6*

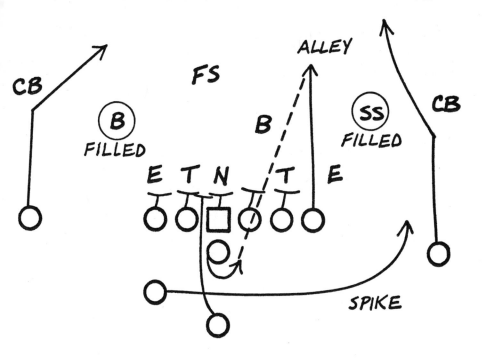

DIAGRAM 12-23: *A Gee-Split, 31 Hum Slant In vs. 52 Reduced*

Hum Modules

Short patterns are thrown from the *Hum* protection. Use *31, 80, 73* and reciprocal actions in addition to a few others. In Diagram 12-23 a *Slant In* from *31 Hum* is shown. Prior to the snap, the quarterback reads the area between the tight end and wide out. If it is not filled, that is where he will make his pass. If it is filled, he looks to the split side; if that is not filled, that is the side to which he passes. If both sides are filled, the quarterback passes to the tight end on the alley when he comes open.

Screens

We have run *Screens* from *Pull* or *Drop* or many backfield actions. The quarterback takes his seven step drop, sets up, looks off downfield, then backs up two more steps and unloads the *Screen* to the receiver. An example of a *Screen* is shown in Diagram 12-24. *Screen* passes are easy to vary. You can make an end or any back a *Screen* receiver if you wish.

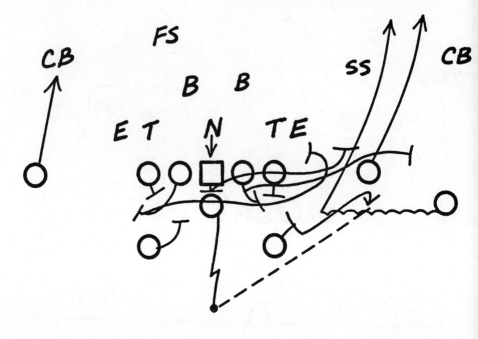

DIAGRAM 12-24: *D Gee String Split Fly, Screen Odd* vs. *5-2*

The blocking for the *Screen* is as for *Drop* or *Pull*, except the center, both guards, and the receiving back lose their blocks three counts after the snap. They form the *Screen* about 10 yards wide of the call side end. The blockers in the *Screen* do not allow anyone to penetrate the *Screen*. The receiver yells "Go" when the ball touches his hands. The outside blocker blocks out, the middle man leads upfield, and the inside man blocks back inside.

A fast *Screen* to a wide receiver or a back running a spike is executed by calling a *Tower*. The guard on the *Tower* side pulls and leads upfield. You usually fill his position, and the remainder of the protection is *Hum*, as shown in Diagram 12-25.

Draws and Sketches

Draws and *Sketches* are in the run modules because they are sometimes combined with a delayed running play. If you wish, you may call any back for the *Draw* or the *Sketch*. The quarter-

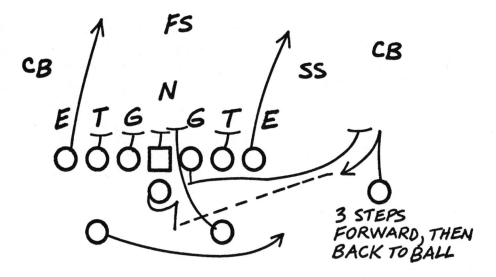

DIAGRAM 12-25: *C Gee 80 Tower Odd* vs. *6-1*

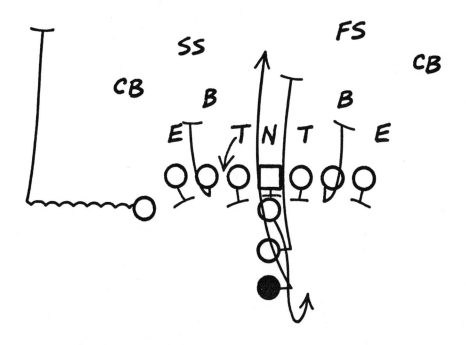

DIAGRAM 12-26: *I Star Float, Tailback Sketch* vs. *5-2 Eagle*

back makes his drop so he can get the ball to the designated back. All backs wait in position for the quarterback with the left arm up in the pocket. The exception to that rule is the quick halfback who makes his pocket in the opposite manner. The back who is not designated as the ball carrier sets up as if to block for one count, and leads upfield on his side of the line. The runner waits patiently for the quarterback to deliver the ball to him, reads the blocking and accelerates through an opening. A tailback *Sketch* is shown in Diagram 12-26.

chapter 13

The Modular Game Plan and Two Golden Minutes

Set up your pre-season practice schedules so that you teach the parts of the Modular Offense that you wish to stress for that given year. Base each year's modular system on the capabilities of your personnel and your general impression of what to expect from your opponents over the complete season.

For each game adjust the Modular Offense to best implement your offense against the opponent's style of defense and the capabilities of his personnel. As the season progresses you will discover that your squad develops certain abilities that will have a great deal to do with the trend that your offense takes as the weeks go by.

A Planning Guide

For use as a planning guide a week's offensive planning is set up as a "war game" to demonstrate the use of the Modular Offense. It is as broad as the coach is creative. Its possibilities expand in direct proportion to the amount you learn about it and the way you use it from week to week.

The game is set up this way. You will play the vaunted Mortonsville Terrors this week. They are a great rival and their team strength is about equal to yours. All things considered, the game is figured as a toss-up. An abstracted scouting report is included in Diagram 13-1. This summary was made from a study of two of their game films, three live scouting reports, and experience in coaching against the Mortonsville coaching staff for the previous two years.

Mortonsville wants to make the big play defensively, and they have succeeded in doing just that a great many times this season. They concede an occasional big play by the offense, but their philosophy is to break their opponents' consistency and not allow them to possess the ball for long periods of time. They also want to create more possibilities for turnovers. They have an all state linebacker and a superb free safety; their other personnel are pretty good, except for some weakness at left end. Only the safeties flop sides according to the defense called or the strength of the offense.

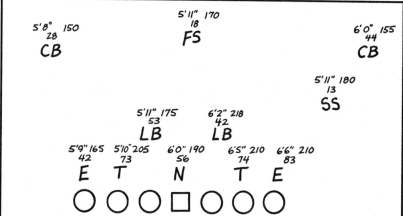

Mortonsville is a basic 52 team. All players remain in position except safeties who flop sides according to strength of the offense. #42 is the best linebacker you will see this year. #18 is a fine defensive back, one of the two or three best you will see. #83 has not done well at defensive end. This team stunts on run downs (breakdowns shown in game plans) three fourths of the time. They do it so well and so often that they demoralize the opponents and break down the offense, robbing it of consistency, and causing turnovers. They have shown some 6-1 on short yardage (RLB goes to RG and N moves to LG, LLB becomes MLB). They often reduce the tackle and end on the split end side. On long yardage, they rarely stunt or blitz, using a 52 with a 3 deep zone. The end away from the SS drops on action passes away from him, or on drop back passes.

DIAGRAM 13-1: Abstracted Mortonsville Scouting Report

They have many stunts involving pressure from the linebackers. They frequently blitz the strong safety. Diagrams 13-2, 13-3, 13-4, and 13-5 illustrate defensive alignments and maneuvers you can expect to face, as well as the mirrors of those defenses. During film study sessions, the coaches discuss some ideas on which offensive modules to combine to make an effective game plan. The head coach and/or offensive coordinator take these ideas and develop them. Subsequently they are presented to a meeting of all the coaches prior to the

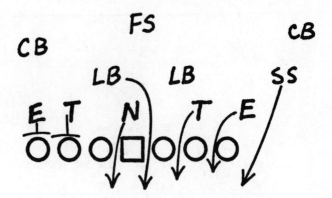

DIAGRAM 13-2: *Blitz* **Combined With** *Slant-LB Stunt*

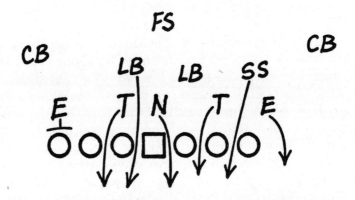

DIAGRAM 13-3: *Eagle Stunt* **Combined With Off Tackle Blitz**

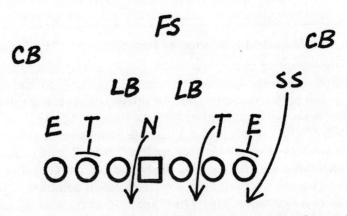

DIAGRAM 13-4: *Full Slant* **Combined With Scraping Linebacker and** *Blitz*

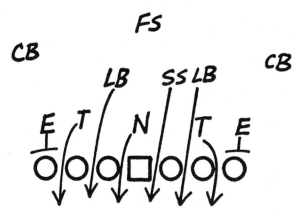

DIAGRAM 13-5: *Double Linebacker Stunt* Combined With Strong Safety Blitz

week's practice. The plan is critiqued by all the coaches and put in final form at the staff meeting. Diagram 13-6 is the Mortonsville game plan. You will be careful about making changes in the game plan after it is submitted to the squad and practiced on Monday. Except in rare cases, any changes are minor and you will eliminate plays rather than add them.

The Running Game

Mortonsville has been very successful with the strong safety blitz. When they use that maneuver, they have a penetrating eight man front for you to block. It is easier to block a seven man front (there are simply fewer of them) so the first consideration is to use your formations in such a way as to reduce that defensive front. Analysis tells you that they do not run the strong safety to the opposite side when the other team changes strength with motion. Their adjustment is to roll the strong safety back to replace the free safety, and to bring the free safety up as an extra defender on the change in strength. This takes them out of the safety blitz. As a result, you use a great deal of *Zip* motion by the Z back, starting him as a wing or slot, then motioning him across the formation. You also use a great deal of shift opposite, starting the Z back as a wing or slot on one side and shifting him to the opposite side. That takes them out of the strong safety blitz, reducing your problems with that maneuver.

In order to deal with the stunts, be careful that you do a good job of stepping to the front side with your offensive line. Offensive linemen who face a bubble (linebacker) will step laterally in order to block the slanting lineman if their assignment is the linebacker and the play is to the outside. If the lineman is not slanting to the inside, our lineman comes off for the linebacker. Mortonsville adjusts their strong safety to your formation strength and not to the wide side of the field, so you want to shift strength into the short side and sweep quickly or toss quickly on your left hash. That enables you to take advantage of their left end and to get the wide side of the field, with their strong safety rolled back to free safety. Rather than trap this team we will pin them, trapping the linebackers...a better idea against their stunts.

The Passing Game

The shifting and motion of your Z back reduces the strong safety blitz and makes your pass protection effective. Mortonsville mixes a three deep zone and quite a bit of man coverage. You usually will see the man coverage in the stunt situations. Take advantage of this coverage by using crossing combination patterns, or misdirection passes, such as *Boots* or *Waggles*, in run situations. In obvious pass situations use some *Flood* against the zone along with some patterns from the *Pulls*. There is one *Drop* play in which the quarterback reads the free safety. Include a draw and a screen to each side.

Restrict the plays and formations. As a guide, limit your formations to from six to nine, and your plays to about 25. You should be selective enough so that you attack the defensive weaknesses with your best weapons.

Special Situations

The scouting report gives us an idea of when you can expect your opponent to be in certain defenses, and you structure the game plan to take advantage of that. This team stunts on the running downs and tends to lay back on the passing downs. You will throw some play fake passes on the run downs and execute runs on some of the passing downs. This increases your chances of making the big play on the run downs, and tends to reduce the chance of turnovers on the long yardage

Distance	Goal	Left Hash	Middle	Right Hash
All 1sts 2nd long 2nd med All shorts	Goal line	A Star-Spl Zip 350 I Gee Opp 62 BI I Gee Opp 63 BI	B Gee Opp 49 Toss B Gee Opp 55 Wham I Pro Opp 64 BI	A North Zip 72 Wham B Gee Opp Spr Odd FI I Gee Opp 73 Base
3rd long 4th med	10	B Gee Opp SO FI	C Gee, Y Pro 81 H	B Gee Opp Spr Odd FI A North Zip SE FI
1st long 2nd med 3rd short 4th short		A Star Spl Zip 33P I Gee Opp 65 BK A Star Spl Zip 350 B Gee Opp 340	I Gee Opp, 71 C I Gee Opp 73 B I Pro Opp 63 BE I Pro Opp 63 BI	C Gee, Y Pro 850 I Pro Opp 64 BI I Gee Opp 70 C
2nd long 3rd long	20	A Star Spl Zip 87B I Gee Opp 65 Spr Str Sq B Gee Opp SO FI	I Pro Opp 64 Spr Str Sq B Gee Opp SO FI B Gee Opp PO TE Delay	I Pro Opp 64 Spr Str Sq C Gee, Y Pro QHB Draw
1st long 2nd med 3rd short 4th short		B Gee Opp 49T B Gee Opp 34 WO Deep Out I Gee Opp 65 BI I Gee Opp 64 BIK	C Gee, Y Pro 87B A Star Spl Zip 54 L A Star Spl Zip 35 WE A Star Spl Zip 33P	A Star Spl FI 54 L I Gee Opp 70C A Star Spl Zip 33P I Gee Opp 64 BIK

Long 8 +   Medium 4 to 7   Short 0 to 3

DIAGRAM 13-6: Mortonsville Game Plan By Situation

Distance	Goal	Left Hash	Middle	Right Hash
2nd long 3rd long	50	B Gee Opp 49T B Gee Opp PO Cor Rel B Gee Opp SO Fl	A Star Spl Zip Drop F/O Even C Gee, Y Pro Screen Even I Gee Opp 65 Spr Flg Bend	B Gee Opp SO Fl A North Zip SE Fl A Star Spl Zip Drop F/O Even
1st long 2nd med 3rd short		B Gee Opp SO Fl B Gee Opp 80P B Gee Opp 55W I Gee Opp 73B	I Gee Opp 65 Spr Str Sq I Gee Opp 65 Bl I Gee Opp 64 Bl	I Pro Opp 62 Bl B Gee Opp 80P I Gee Opp 64 Bl A North Zip 54W
2nd long 3rd long	20	C Gee, Y Pro 81 H C Gee, Y Pro 87B A North Zip Screen Odd	B Gee Opp PO Curl Fl C Gee, Y Pro QHB Draw	I Pro Opp 64 Spr Str Sq A North Zip PE Deep Out
All sits	Goal line	A North Zip 87B A Star Spl Zip 350 B Gee Opp 55W I Gee Opp 63 Bl	A North Zip 72W A North Zip 55W I Pro Opp 62 Bl I Pro Opp 71 C	C Gee, Y Pro 48T I Pro Opp 64 Blk A Star Spl Fl 54L I Gee Opp 65 Bl

Long 8 +   Medium 4 to 7   Short 0 to 3

DIAGRAM 13-6: Mortonsville Game Plan By Situation (cont.)

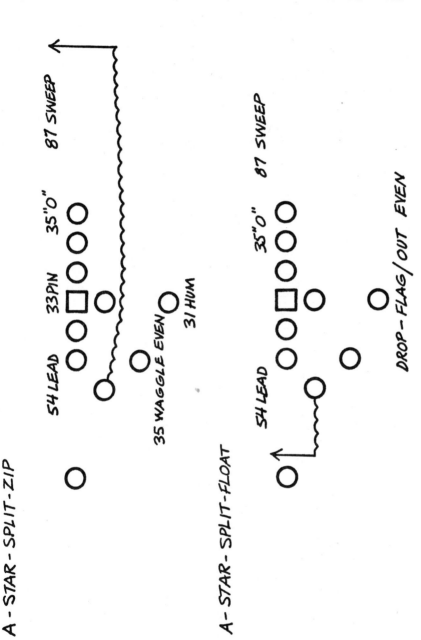

DIAGRAM 13-6: Mortonsville Game Plan By Formation

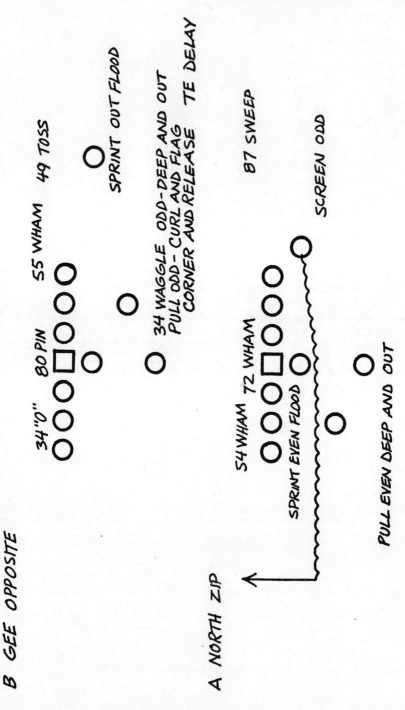

DIAGRAM 13-6: Mortonsville Game Plan By Formation (cont.)

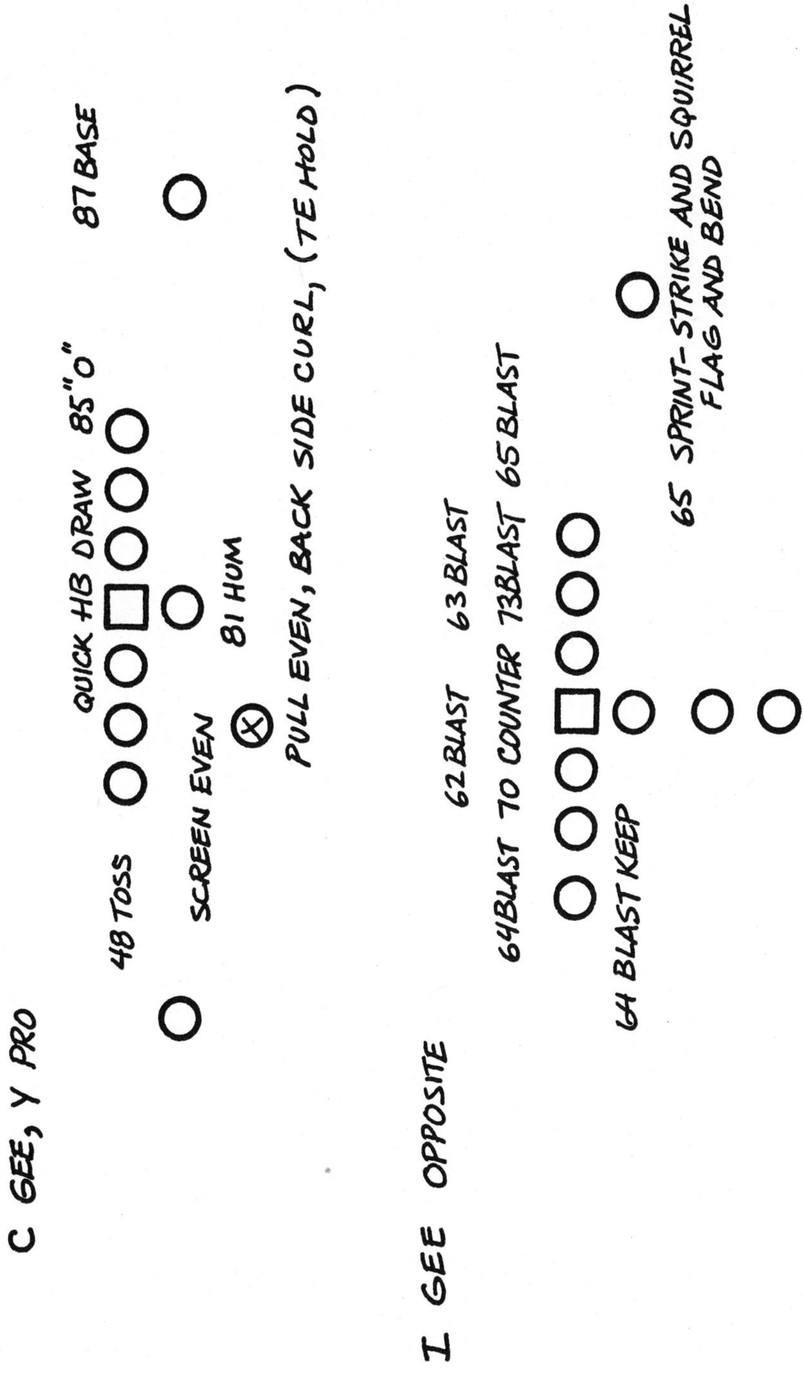

C GEE, Y PRO

48 TOSS   QUICK HB DRAW   85 "O"   87 BASE

SCREEN EVEN

81 HUM

PULL EVEN, BACK SIDE CURL, (TE HOLD)

I GEE OPPOSITE

62 BLAST   63 BLAST

64 BLAST TO COUNTER   73 BLAST   65 BLAST

64 BLAST KEEP

6S SPRINT- STRIKE AND SQUIRREL
FLAG AND BEND

DIAGRAM 13-6: Mortonsville Game Plan By Formation (cont.)

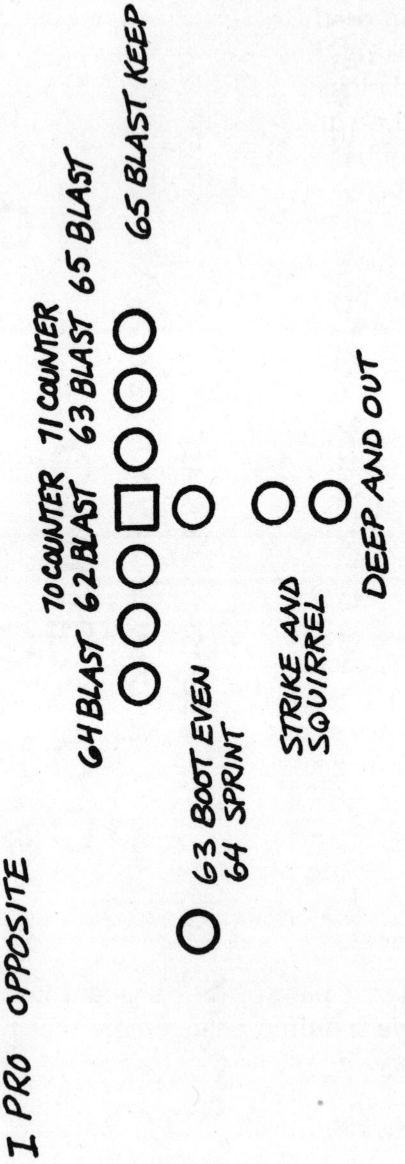

I PRO OPPOSITE

65 BLAST KEEP

71 COUNTER

70 COUNTER   65 BLAST

64 BLAST   62 BLAST   63 BLAST

DEEP AND OUT

STRIKE AND
SQUIRREL

63 BOOT EVEN
64 SPRINT

DIAGRAM 13-6: Mortonsville Game Plan By Formation (cont.)

situations. You want to take their game away from them and control the ball by establishing a consistent running game. The only way you can do that is to make sure you get quality practice time in blocking their 52 stunts. If you cover all defenders on the front, and block effectively, you will have long gains and consistency in the running game.

Determine which situations are long yardage, medium yardage, and short yardage by analysis of the film summaries and scouting reports. Prepare your offense so you will be able to block all the fronts for all your plays. Mortonsville uses a 65 on the goal line (Diagram 13-7) in which they try to keep the middle linebacker free. Hit and run your center and guard and get off tackle against that defense. Throw the *Sprint Odd Flood* against that defense, with the Z back curling at the end line (Diagram 13-8). In very short goal line situations the opponent blitzes the safeties; we are prepared to handle that blitz as shown in Diagram 13-9.

Calling the Play

You will develop a system that suits you best for calling plays. It is good to have a coach in the press box who phones the plays down to the bench. He has the game plan in front of him in order to make notes easily. He also has an excellent view of the action on the playing field. You can use visual signals from the bench to get the plays into the game. It is faster and more accurate than sending in a messenger and allows the freedom of not sending in a substitute when you wish to call a play.

Halftime Adjustments

The fan often has a picture of a brilliant coach as one who makes remarkable halftime adjustments that turn a losing effort into a victory. If you find yourself making major adjustments at halftime every week, you are doing a poor job of preparation. Approach halftime as a period in which to eliminate the ineffective parts of your game plan and to focus on things that you have practiced during the week and which showed some potential in the first half. There is a time to break every rule, but try not to put in new plays or make radical changes.

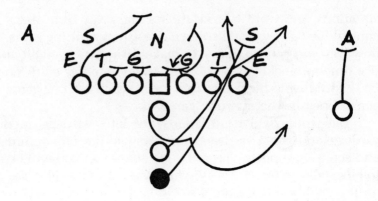

DIAGRAM 13-7: *I Gee, 65 Blast vs. 65 Goal Line*

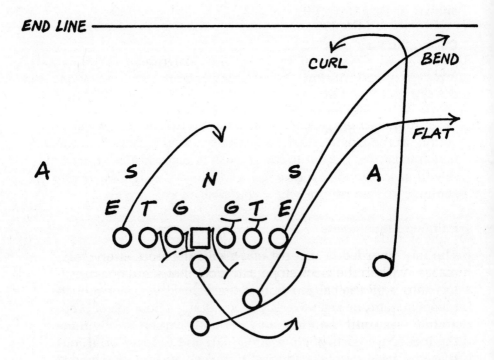

DIAGRAM 13-8: *B Gee Opposite, Sprint Odd Flood vs. 65 Goal Line*

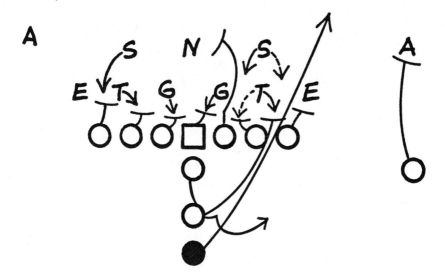

DIAGRAM 13-9: *I Gee Opposite, 65 Blast vs. Blitzing Goal Line 65*

An occasional adjustment in a blocking assignment or pass route, or the substitution of a blocking module for a similar module on a certain play is about as far as you should go with changes. The most important purposes of the halftime break are to clear up confusion on the part of the players and to reinforce the good things they did in the first half.

Two Golden Minutes

The final two minutes of the half or the game can be productive for the Modular Offense. It is a special circumstance in which discipline is needed to run plays and save the clock. Everyone must know when the clock stops. The clock stops and does not start again until the ball is snapped for a charged time out, an incomplete pass, or an out-of-bounds play. The clock stops and does not start until the ball is spotted for first downs, official's time out, or a penalty following a play in which the clock would not stop. All players must discipline themselves to call time out on direction from the bench. The quarterback is responsible for keeping the squad hustling and not wasting valuable seconds. The squad must keep its poise during this period.

To conserve time you may call two plays in the same huddle. Do not shift or use motion in the two minute drill. The quarterback can call the play from the line of scrimmage. If it is not fourth down, the quarterback can stop the clock by signalling his team to align on the ball with the Z back flanked to the short side. On the spot the quarterback sets his team and has the squad execute a quick out pass to the Z back. If the Z back is clean the pass is completed. If the defense has any chance of breaking up the quick out pass, the quarterback throws the ball over the receiver's head.

Make certain you devote practice time to the two minute drill. Those two golden minutes will pay dividends.

Trying the Modular Offense

The modular concept gives you a starting base. Your creativity and contributions to its actual use make it your own specially tailored plan of attack. You will experience the joy and the occasional frustrations of football creativity. It is an experience you will never forget.

INDEX

FOOTBALL'S MODULAR OFFENSE

Now you can keep your opponent's defensive front from reading your plays...stop their pass rush...and take the power out of their perimeter coverage.

You can do all this—and do it easily—with FOOTBALL'S MODULAR OFFENSE, a multiple offense that gives you the tools needed to put together a flexible attack.

From an exciting variation of the Trap that gives an excellent blocking setup for delayed plays...to the Post pass route that gives receivers many new options—you get a storehouse of diverse maneuvers that will cut down on interceptions, attack the off-tackle hole, and contain defensive coverage to the backside.

Considering the confusion it will cause your opponents, the Modular is strikingly simple in structure and a breeze to coach.

The Modular uses just a few basic blocking...running...and passing fundamentals as its foundation.

But what makes the Modular unique is that it gives you specific ways to use these fundamentals in various combinations that produce an aggressive, challenging offense.

You get a variety of sets at your fingertips ...motions...backfield flow patterns...pass action...and pass routes that constantly attack